LIGHT OF MY HEART
A Journey With Amma

A loving heart is filled with an ocean
Cradling existence gently in its undulating waves.

Rumi

I dedicate this book to Amma, the Light in my heart,
and to my daughters Andrea and Lisa.

Mata Amritanandamayi Center
San Ramon, CA 94583, United States

LIGHT OF MY HEART
A Journey with Amma

By Anna Prabha Dreier
annapra.dreier@gmail.com

Published by:
Mata Amritanandamayi Center
P.O. Box 613
San Ramon, CA 94583
United States

In India:
www.amritapuri.org
inform@amritapuri.org

In Europe:
www.amma-europe.org

In US:
www.amma.org

CONTENTS

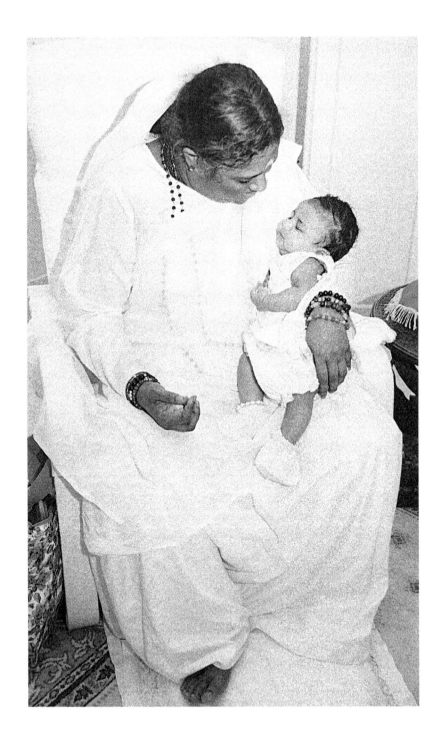

1

Prologue

Only when the waves subside
can you see the reflection of the sun in the water.
In the same way, you can only see the Self
when your thought waves become calm.

Amma

A blank sheet of paper lies in front of me, waiting to accept the first words of this book. It forces my attention to the present moment even as my thoughts fly to the future. They are busy lining up several sheets of paper next to this empty one on the table. They fill these sheets with words, come up with titles, put pictures in place and shatter my concentration with such force that I lose myself and no longer know what I would have liked to write to begin with.

What an unfortunate game it is that my mind plays daily! It loves to play like this, not only when I am trying to write a book. Does it not already transport me to the stove when I am at the market buying vegetables? Does it not already picture me at the concert hall when I am getting a new dress sewn for the occasion? Amma says it is my job to break the control of the mind and make it my faithful servant.

Young Amma writing

I am still working on this difficult project that consumes my entire attention from second to second. I hope that writing this book will help my mind to focus and, as Amma encourages us to, I hope one day to hold the remote control of my mind firmly in my hands.

A hint about how I can do this comes to me from the past. I remember a similar situation, something that happened long ago. I was in the garden of a Zen center and had just finished bowing down to the earth. In front of me was a large round piece of land that had once been covered with gravel. It was now thickly overgrown with grassy weeds that had burst out between each stone. I was supposed to pull out the weeds, pull them out till the large piece of land that measured several square meters was again transformed into its original state – a seating area furnished with tables and chairs.

Thinking about my assignment, I was completely discouraged as I looked around, taking in all the weeds. As I silently knelt down on the land, I suddenly realized: "Look at only one single plant, at the one that you are touching and trying to pull out at this moment."

Soon my energy was focused. My hands touched the earth and the first weed. Carefully I pulled it out, saw the fine roots, shook off the mud and placed it in the basket next to me. I repeated this process the next minute, the next hour and hundreds of times more that day, the next day and so on till the gravel-filled piece of land revealed itself.

And now this empty white sheet of paper lies before me, ready to accept my words and pictures. Countless sheets of paper will follow the first one, and I will try very hard to focus my attention on only one sheet at a time – on the one that lies in front of me at this moment.

May Amma help us always to remain centered on one paper from the book of our life – on the one being written in this present moment.

2

BIOGRAPHY

There is no effort involved in the Master's presence.
He is simply there.
In his divine energy, everything happens spontaneously.

Amma

On the day of the Karthika star in the year 1953, a small girl was born into a fishing family on the peninsula of Parayakadavu, in the South Indian state of Kerala. The newborn named Sudhamani, ambrosial jewel, smiled after she was born, and to the astonishment of her parents and siblings, showed unusual signs as she grew older. Even at six months old Sudhamani was able to walk and speak. At a tender age, she started composing and singing heart-rending spiritual songs (*bhajans*) dedicated to the divine.

The villagers recount that even then Sudhamani would lovingly take care of the neighbors whenever they were in need. She consoled the sad, looked after the sick and brought the hungry food to eat. Without her parents' permission she took rice and lentils from home and gave them to the poor. She also used to take a portion of the milk and give it to them, and mix water in the rest so no one in the family would notice. One day she even stole some of her mother's jewelry and gave it to a starving family so that they could sell it and use that money to buy food and other necessities. Her parents did not show the slightest understanding for her actions; on the contrary, they were irritated by what she did.

With her compassionate ways, Sudhamani soon won the hearts of the people in her village. However, for her own family she became something of a problem. They could not understand her intense, deep, meditative states, or her habit of dancing ecstatically in public. Due to their ignorance, her parents punished their daughter many times. Yet, no one could dissuade Sudhamani from caring for the poor. Once when someone was very sad, she spontaneously hugged and comforted this person to the chagrin of her parents and relatives. It was a complete taboo in the Indian culture for a twelve-year old girl to hug strangers so intimately, including older men and people of other castes. "There was a time," Amma said later, "when people would throw stones at me when I walked through the village." Sudhamani was not dissuaded by all this criticism.

When Sudhamani turned nine her mother fell ill, and she had to give up school to take care of her large family. She became a servant of sorts to the Idamannels: she cooked for her parents

Neighbours with Amma in early days

12

and seven siblings, cleaned the house, and washed and fed the animals, working every day from dawn till midnight.

Even though she had to work so hard and her family did not understand her, Sudhamani spent many hours at night in deep meditation and intense prayer. She adored Krishna, whose picture she always carried with her. She chanted his name without interruption, and at the age of twenty-two revealed a glimpse of the bliss of Self-Realization within her, of unity with the divine.

She was fully established in this state of union with the all-encompassing Love and Compassion of the divine. Her condition could no longer be denied and the news spread that she radiated an unearthly Love. Many people gathered around her to find consolation and seek her advice. Because there was no other place, they met with Sudhamani on the beach to spend some time in her hallowed presence and be comforted. Sudhamani did not care for social conventions and did what she had to out of love and compassion. For her, all people were equal. Her acceptance of everyone and her compassionate embrace was a strong message against societal exclusions based on caste barriers, nationality

and gender. "There is no key with which one can lock up love," she said. Because of her unusual ways she also had many opponents. In order to protect his daughter, her father, Sugunanandan, converted his cowshed into a temple of sorts, where Sudhamani could receive the ever-growing number of people who came to her. By and by, spiritual seekers from all corners of India came to know of this young fisher girl who could transport them into a state of deep peace. Some of them did not want to leave the young Sudhamani, and stayed back in the village to be in her presence. Recognizing the unique qualities of this young girl, they requested that she become their spiritual master. One of these young men, now called Swami Turiyamritananda Puri, gave Amma the name "Mata Amritanandamayi", the Mother of Immortal Bliss, and the other young men, today swamis as well, agreed to the suggestion.

In the year 1979, to the astonishment of her family and the village, the first seekers from the west also came to the secluded community by the Arabian Sea. To give her some privacy, these seekers built her a little hut thatched with coconut palm leaves. This marked the beginnings of the Amritapuri Ashram of today. (The ashram has grown to include housing for its over 3,000 permanent residents and thousands of guests, as well as an allopathic hospital, an ayurvedic hospital, and various shops that serve the needs of people who come. There are several facilities for meditation, yoga and such, as well as a large central temple. Nearby on the mainland stands one of the five campuses of Amrita University, which includes a medical research center in the city of Kochi.)

Amma had already been traveling to various parts of India, when in 1987, she began international tours as well. She was now commonly called 'Amma' (Mother) and carried her message of compassion and humble service and love to the entire world.

Today Amma has inspired thousands of people from all walks of life. Ministers, scientists, educators, film stars, the poorest of the poor as well as the richest of the rich, all seek her advice and counsel. She uplifts and transforms through her embrace, her spiritual wisdom and the projects of her worldwide charitable organization, which consists primarily of volunteers. The countless projects they undertake support the needy regardless of religion, social status or caste. This NGO, Embracing the World (ETW), enjoys advisory status for the Economic and Social Council of the United Nations, as well as the UN Department for Public Information.

When asked where she gets the energy to help this sea of humanity and to build and lead a massive humanitarian organization, she answers:

"Where there is true Love there is no effort."

Amma in Toulon. France

3

LIVE YOUR LIFE

My soul is a bird that flies.
Fly, bird of heaven, bird of earth
Into the world and give it your song
Without attachments, fly and sing.

Prabha

If you are born with a heart full of longing, your life will be a search for home-coming to a fullness that is both silence and true belonging. Your path will not be easy. You will have to swim against the current, plunge into depths, let go of your likes and dislikes, and experience pain and loneliness. The needle of your inner compass will not point to the conventional, rather it will point towards the eternal in your heart. It will point to the path of the great mystery that you can intuit in those rare moments the universe offers you. Whatever you may experience in life, it is up to you whether you want to remain in love and take the steps that will finally bring you back home.

There are only a few maps that show the way to the kingdom of Oneness and Unity. My map is Amma. She let me find her.

I had been searching for Amma as long as I can remember. But please, do not think that I was looking for a petite Indian lady in a white dress. Rather, I was looking for a state of mind in which all thoughts would be silent. In this state I could experience peace and love, a sense of belonging and connectedness with the entire creation. Even as a child I used to seek lonely, out of the way spots. I called them my 'hideouts' where I could be absolutely alone, all by myself. I found such spots, for example, under the antique sewing table in my parental home, behind the heavy curtains in the living room, or in the large trunk for firewood in my grandmother's kitchen. The forests, however, were my favorite place. There I built little huts and shelters using twigs and branches and settled down just to BE. I sat in the stillness of these hideouts and let myself sink into a state of no thought, and slowly be carried into a space where everything was perfect as it was, and I was enveloped in a feeling of great bliss. I felt unconditional love. Even though my family had tried to portray God as a stern, punishing being up in heaven, in these moments I knew that God was my best friend. Yes, even my most intimate kin.

I was a difficult child. Difficult to raise and even more difficult to understand. As I grew older I longed for nothing else than to be like everyone else. I could not share what I experienced in those moments in my hideouts with anyone, not even my parents. Thus, I sacrificed what was so precious to me in order to integrate myself into a normal life as a young adult. That was how I lost myself.

I picked up various skills and jobs, married, had two wonderful children and led a life that many of my friends envied. One could say that I had situated myself extremely well on this planet. I was using my talents in the best possible way, but I was a restless person. I longed for nourishment, for fulfillment, for peace. Nothing that I came across could fill the emptiness created by this longing.

Spirituality began to interest me. I tried everything – Zen, Christianity, Buddhism and belonged for many years to the circle of a Shaman. I meditated, read, discussed, and attended workshops with like-minded people. Slowly my inner world woke up again. There were brief moments when I experienced the Truth that I had forgotten. My longing grew; it possessed my being and fought against the meaninglessness of my life. My children were grown up, my husband found another woman, and Amma came into my life at just the right time.

I saw her for the first time in the Swiss mountains in the summer of 1989. A girlfriend who had already visited Amma in India took me to the large old building of a spiritual center situated in the majestic mountains. Only a couple of hundred people were in this temple dedicated to Babaji of Haidakhan. The atmosphere was playful and light, almost hippie-like with many young families

and children in pretty summer clothing. At that time there were no lines, no tokens, no or time cards. A wonderful peace hung in the air during the pauses between the bhajans. Sometimes one could hear Amma laugh and say a few words in a foreign language.

She sat at the edge of a small stage and hugged for a long time each of those who knelt before her. We all took in this sacred scene from very near, closely watching Amma's shining eyes and her captivating smile. We saw how sometimes while hugging she would sing along with the swamis, all the while rocking the devotee in her arms to the music, as a mother would rock a baby in the cradle.

I, too, got in line and moved closer to Amma. Time and space lost meaning, my mind became still. My body became relaxed in the inner stillness created by the cessation of thoughts. I let myself be filled with Amma's energy that pulsed through me, and had the feeling that I was at the best place on this planet at the very best time. I remember almost flowing into Amma's arms and closing my eyes. During this first embrace I relived those precious moments of stillness and awareness from my childhood. I was loved, protected and receptive, wide open as the universe. I could hear Amma whisper something in my ear that sounded like "Bonsoir, bonsoir," which means good evening in French. The afternoon sun was shining brightly outside on that hot summer day. Yet I repeated "Bonsoir, bonsoir" back to Amma without looking at her, not realizing that she was whispering "Shiva, Shiva" into my ears. All of me turned into a highly sensitive receptivity and I knew that she was the ONE. She was one with everything, one with the whole universe and one with me. I was home and my heart was at peace.

However, on the third day of the five-day retreat everything changed. A powerful restlessness and distrust overcame me. Yes, me – who had danced without a care in Amma's energy until then. What was wrong with my mind? Had my ego gone crazy? My thoughts were running amok and overwhelmed me. They painted a desolate picture in my mind and whispered: "You are letting yourself be trapped. You have fallen into the spider's web. You will be eaten and chewed up." A bitter struggle ensued in me. My mind imagined itself to be in danger and did everything to pull me away from the miraculous experience of the heart. "You are a Shaman woman. Do not enter the world of this Indian lady. You will be totally lost." My thoughts bombarded me and I stood on the inner battlefield completely exhausted. Several times I stood in the distant doorway and watched the hum of activity around Amma. I would also stand in front of the bathroom mirror,

Schweibenalp, Switzerland 1992

looking at my reflection and repeating: "You are a Shaman, yes, remember you are a Shaman."

Irritated and restless, I sought out my small tent. My inner world was no longer the same. Everything wonderful that had happened to me now came up against self-erected fences, and touched sleeping dreams and fears. My inner world was now chaotic. These thoughts gathered force and momentum, were totally incomprehensible, and attacked everything that only a few days before had brought me deep fulfillment. Why could my mind not let go of my self-made image? Or was my intellect perhaps right? Was good sense trying to warn me?

I was just about to lie down on my mat when a voice clearly spoke: "Truth carries weight." My body immediately became heavy as if to support the words I just heard. A complete relaxation overcame me. The battle in my mind ceased, the thoughts disappeared into nothingness and every cell in my body filled with a pulsating life. I was again in Amma's presence, protected in an invisible embrace. I sat completely still with eyes closed, just as I had as a child, and let transformation take place, the transformation from a Shaman woman to a child of Amma.

That evening, this newly born Amma's child took her first steps into the tent where Amma was giving *darshan*. She effortlessly found a space in the third row and sat down on the jute sack that served as a seat to listen to Amma's words and the bhajans that followed. I felt so close to Amma. A feeling of intimacy

Schweibenalp 1992

washed over me and I longed for her embrace. During the closing prayers I saw how the people formed two lines to Amma's left and right to go up for darshan. They stood in silent expectation, waiting for their turn to be in her arms.

I stayed seated on my spot and watched how Amma reached out to each person with supreme love, hugged them closely, whispered in their ears, and touched their foreheads with sandalwood paste. Soon it seemed like the people in front of me magically disappeared and there I was, directly in front of Amma, who held her arms open to me.

I lay yet again with closed eyes in Amma's arms to forget myself in a feeling of deep security. I was about to let myself be carried away when a sudden, intense stillness descended around me and in me. I felt as if I were in a vacuum chamber filled with a powerful vibration. I came to a complete standstill, both internally and externally. Confused about what was happening, I opened my eyes and looked straight into Amma's dark, glowing, tender eyes, which looked straight at me and seemed to say: "There, this is the Truth that has weight. Don't try to leave. Come with me on the journey to the great mystery in your heart. Trust me and I will lead you." I followed her.

When I saw Amma for the first time,
My eyes gazed into hers.
But my eyes were no longer my eyes,
They were my heart, and Amma gazed into my heart.
But my heart was no longer my heart,
It was the Universe
And Amma's eyes and my eyes met.

Prabha

On a fiord in Sweden

Your true nature is like the sky, not the clouds.
It is like the ocean, not the waves.
The sky and the ocean are like pure consciousness.
Clouds and waves come and go,
but the sky and the ocean remain
as the substratum of their existence.

Amma

4

YOU ARE A KING EAGLE

A hen once lay brooding on an eagle's egg, which happened to be among its own eggs. The eagle hatched and grew up with the chickens, scratching and searching for worms in the soil. Growing up, he was completely identified with his existence as an ordinary farmyard cock.

One day, an eagle soaring in the sky happened to see our Cock-eagle among a group of hens picking up worms on the ground. Amazed, he decided to bring his brother out of delusion and approached him one day when he was alone. But Cock-eagle was afraid of the big bird and wanted to run away. "I am your friend," said Sky-eagle." I have to tell you something very important."

He explained to Cock-eagle that he was not an ordinary farmyard chicken, but a mighty eagle like himself, who had the ability to soar up in the sky.

Sky-eagle said, "You don't belong to the earth. You belong to the vast infinite sky. Come with me and experience the bliss of soaring through the air. You can do it because you are just like me. You have the same powers that I have."

In this way Sky-eagle tried to persuade Cock-eagle. At first Cock-eagle was full of disbelief. He even thought that it might be a trap of some sort.

But Sky-eagle was determined not to give up. Slowly he gained Cock-eagle's confidence, and Cock-eagle followed him to a nearby lake. They stood at the edge of the water and Sky-eagle said to Cock-eagle: "Now look into the water. Look at your reflection and see the close resemblance between the two of us."

Cock-eagle looked into the clear, still water. He looked and looked, and he could not believe his eyes. It was the first time in his life that he had seen his real image, and now he knew that he did not look like a chicken. He gained a great deal of self-confidence, and he obeyed unconditionally all the instructions Sky-eagle gave him. At first Cock-eagle had some difficulty in rising from the ground. But soon the two eagles could be seen gracefully soaring together through the sky.

Amma is our Mother Sky-eagle, showing us day after day who we are in reality: Divine beings in human bodies.

When we are identified with the body, mind and intellect, we are living like Cock-eagle, but within each of us lies the treasure of the Self. The Compassion, Love and Light of Sky-eagle are waiting to spread their wings and soar through us into the world.

Walking through the door of the chalet in Schweibenalp

5

DEVI BHAVA PETALS

*Pure Love springs from an insatiable hunger
and a profound desire.
Love is your true nature. Your real being is divine Love
and nothing can exist that is not a manifestation of it.*

Amma

Amma had found me, and I felt accepted. There was a celebration in my heart. Spring had come to my soul's garden. A thousand tender flowers blossomed. Intoxicated by their fragrance I forgot everything I had said to my friend before we drove out to meet Amma. I had told her categorically: "I only want a Master who can also be strict. Someone who is always only loving and sweet can do nothing for me."

I now danced in Amma's Love, a happy child without a care in the world, fully unaware that Amma knew exactly what I had said a few weeks before about the right Master for me. How should I have known this? I had no idea about the all-encompassing nature of a Being like Amma.

She knew everything about me that she needed to know and picked a Devi Bhava night to seek me out, to bring me close to her and remind me of my wish for a strict Guru. It was a fascinating

Devi Bhava night for me. An immense power and otherworldly beauty emanated from Amma. In a colorful silk sari and crown, she looked like the personification of the divine energy of Devi, the godly mother. Her body vibrated and the anklets on her feet jingled. I saw how the devotees approached her on their knees, how she pulled each person into her lap and embraced them with all her heart. How she whispered something in their ears, dabbed sandalwood paste on their forehead, consoled, soothed, encouraged and healed. In her lap each person was equal and secure in the presence of boundless Love. Rays of compassion shone from her eyes and all her movements arose gracefully from an invisible center. She was a sacred gift to humanity, incarnated for all those who were suffering, seeking and thirsting. A dam broke in me, and my tears flowed silently in the stream of her Love.

She was the one I had been waiting for all my life without even knowing it. I was ready to take a *mantra* and create an unbreakable bond with her. I took my place in the seemingly unending line that snaked all the way outside the tent. How difficult it was to wait there for two hours, even though the night was warm, the sky was full of stars and the mountains circled us protectively. It was impossible to wait outside knowing that she sat inside, and

I longed to be in her physical presence. "It is a test," I said to myself. "One must deserve this treasure." I waited and waited and let myself be tested on the subject 'patience' till finally it was my turn to enter into the light of Amma's presence. "Who is your favorite deity?" asked a swami clad in yellow, and I answered that currently my deity list was empty. I would prefer a female deity, I answered and kneeled down to the right of Amma's chair. The swami spoke to Amma who looked at me intently, pulled my head towards her and whispered a few words in my ear that I had never heard before, but whose sounds awoke an ancient world within me. These new sounds spread around inside of me as if they wanted to take possession.

The swami indicated that Amma wanted me to sit next to her and repeat my mantra three times. She pointed to a spot right next to her chair. Then she placed flower petals in my hand and the swami gave me a small slip of paper. I was to read my mantra out loud, and after reciting its last word, offer the flower petals. I did my very best to do the impossible. My lips formed the strange

words, my voice articulated the syllables, and my hands somehow managed to offer the flower petals at the same time. Amma
attentively followed everything I was saying and doing, corrected
me, enunciated the mantra clearly and smiled in amusement at
my clumsiness. She took on the role of the Universal Mother
and transformed me into a small ignorant schoolchild. I had the
feeling of being a complete beginner, and that was exactly what
Amma wanted.

Devi Bhava petals

My mind was still, open and receptive. The wonderful goings
on around Amma, the flow of her Love, the light in her eyes, the
sound of her voice, the anklets on her feet, the splendor of her
sari, her crown, the colors, the music from the swamis, all of
this swirled inside of me like an intoxicating dance. Every cell in
my body danced. After everyone present was embraced, Amma
got up ceremoniously and walked slowly to the front edge of the
stage. From a basket that a lady held out to her, she repeatedly
took handfuls of petals and threw them forcefully into crowds
of devotees in the tent. I could feel the petals on my skin. I was

laughing and dancing. To me it seemed as if the petals changed to snowflakes falling in slow motion from the sky.

I became a child, dancing and catching snowflakes, when suddenly I felt as if my right cheek had been cut by a knife. A searing pain spread over my face. Quickly touching my cheek with my hand, I expected to see blood. But to my surprise there was no blood, yet I still felt wounded. Who had done this to me?

I looked around to find the culprit and saw that all eyes were happily fixed on Amma. I had completely forgotten about her physical form in that shower of petals. I felt her in everything, in the petals that had turned to snowflakes, and the sky from which they fell. She was in all of us, and in our happiness, too. As if waking from a trance, I looked at the stage and directly into Amma's eyes.

For me, these eyes were no longer smiling. Amma's face was dark, and around her lips played a serious smile. I stood rooted to the spot. Had Amma thrown a handful of flowers so forcefully at me that the fine petals could inflict sharp wounds? Yes, that must have been it. Amma stood there looking at me and appearing to say: "Here you have the spiritual teacher you wanted, one who is not only loving but also strict. One who can make you happy with flower petals and also hurt you with them."

It seemed to me that Amma now transformed before my very eyes into a divine Being. She shone like a *murti*, an Indian statue of a deity in a temple. This Being gazed at me from a world to which I had no access.

The curtains of the temple closed suddenly, the music stopped, and someone requested me to sit down with others in a circle to receive further instructions about my mantra. But what did I do? I rushed to my tent, broke it down in a hurry, found two youngsters who drove me down the mountain, climbed into my car in the parking lot and prepared to flee – to flee from that which pulled at every fiber in my being and told me that I would never be the same Anna again. A lake lay on my way home, and as I came up to it, the first rays of sunlight had just touched the water. It was early morning, and I found myself alone in Nature that was just opening her eyes to the morning sun. I parked my car on the shores of the lake and swam upon the sunrays reflecting in the water all the way out into its cool depths.

Later I sat on a large stone. Near me a couple of flower petals floated on the water, letting me know that everything I had experienced the night before was not a dream. I held the small note from the swami in my hand and recited my mantra just as Amma had taught me. And it felt as if the mountains, the lake, the sky and the sun would vibrate and respond to the sound of these ancient words of humanity.

I finally drove back home and spent many hours tossing and turning sleeplessly in bed before I returned at sunset back to the mountains and to Amma. The swamis were singing when I entered the hall, and I suddenly felt so welcome. Amma was embracing, embracing everyone, even me, her happily returned lost child!

When the program was over, she took leave of us and the picturesque spot in the mountains. The vehicle in which she sat moved slowly, and she stretched her hand out through the window

so that the devotees could touch it. I stood alone in the darkness of the forest as she drove past. Our hands touched, and a pair of glittering eyes met mine.

Then she was gone. Yet she was still there with me. I could feel her touch. She was not just the body of an Indian lady clad in white. She stayed back with me as Love, a power that made me blossom and gave my life new direction. The various little rivulets that were wandering around in my inner landscape were now, thanks to her, joined together as one single stream. And this stream continues to grow and flows incessantly towards its goal, towards unity with the ocean.

The Kali Temple under construction

6

To Amritapuri

Be still my heart, be still
In your depths I hark for Mother's song
And spread my arms to dance in Love.

Prabha

My life in India began in January 1990 when an old Air India plane landed at the small airport in Trivandrum, and I set off in search of Amma's ashram, an interminably long ride that lasted several hours.

There was only one way to get to this sacred spot, and my aging taxi driver spent over half a day trying to find it. Sitting in the back seat of the old Ambassador car, I showed everyone whom my helpless chauffeur stopped to ask for assistance, a white piece of paper with the address and a picture of Amma on it. I couldn't understand a single word of what was said. I only noticed that some shook their head, which in India meant 'no,' and others nodded their head, which I guessed had to mean 'yes.' Sometimes someone would climb into the car, like an uninvited guest, and climb out again after a couple of kilometers. Some people we asked for help would point in the exact opposite direction. One smiling young man tore Amma's picture off of the address slip. All in all, everyone seemed to be more interested in my Western *madamma* (foreign woman) face than in Amma's temple. I would have lost all hope, had it not been for my firm conviction that Amma knew I was coming. She was waiting for me!

The ride along the dusty country road, shared by pedestrians, handcarts, bullock carts, cows, bicycles, cars and buses, everyone maneuvering around each other in crazy, unimaginable ways, seemed endless. I clung to the hope that at least the general direction in which we were driving had to be right.

We were indeed headed the right way because the driver suddenly pointed to a street sign. The same name was on the slip of paper with the Ashram's address on it that I was clutching in my hand. He immediately turned into a narrow dirt road, which led us through a simple village landscape set amidst coconut groves, past colorful temples and water lotuses blooming in ponds.

Men sat around in front of simple shops, which they closed with wooden shutters at dusk. Women carried shining metal water jars they had filled from the communal water tap near the road, and children sat in open shelters studying their lessons.

The road came to an abrupt end, and across the wide strip of backwaters I saw my destination. The small *mandapams* of the temple roof towered over the coconut palms in whose shade Amma's abode and the houses of the fisher-folk lay.

Simple boats were tied to the shore of the backwater, which itself looked like a wide river. A boatman waved, somebody reached for my luggage, and soon I was standing as the main attraction in a small boat, which the boatman pushed across the water with a long pole. "*Saipe*," (foreigner) I heard women in colorful saris and men in checked *dhotis* say to one another. Everyone stole glances at me. They were giggling and loudly, speculating among themselves who I might be, and where I came from. I stood there amidst my new neighbors in the boat that was ferrying me to the other shore, and tried my level best to maintain a semblance of equanimity, not to mention my balance.

I was fully aware that I was experiencing a symbolic event. In the Indian scriptures it is said that we are born to cross over

Crossing the backwaters

the Ocean of Samsara. This journey would take us from the life we experience here in the world through our limited mind to a life in the realm of the Self. Now it was my turn, and here I was, crossing the symbolic ocean of this picturesque backwater, standing curious and excited in the boat of a ferryman in a red dhoti.

Amma's large temple was still under construction. The ashram had not yet been named Amritapuri when I arrived there with my few belongings and stood before that impressive structure. I wanted to stay for three months. I stayed for seventeen years!

Darshan was already over when I climbed the steps to the small shop where I had to register my arrival. It was run by a Western resident, who showed me my space in the large dormitory in the temple, the Kali Dorm. She also acquainted me with the dress code – ankle length clothes, and a shawl over the blouse for modesty. I purchased two sets and, dressed in one of them, I took my first steps in Amma's Indian world. It was a wonderful feeling to be like a child on a journey of discovery. Everything was new, and my mind could not label it. I just looked out in amazement.

Daily chores at the backwaters

Expansive backwaters and small lakes separated houses where the fishermen in their hitched up dhotis waded, threw out their rudimentary nets and lured the fish out of their hiding places with loud hand claps. Simple houses, mostly made out of palm fronds, were scattered over the sands. Grandmothers sat at their thresholds watching the scantily clad children, while women in long nighties made of printed Indian cotton cooked food and washed dishes in the open behind the homes.

And then there was the ocean! Large, ancient fishing boats rested on dark fine sands. Fishermen worked on their nets and played cards afterwards. The stretch of land on which Amma's ashram rested was hardly 600 meters wide, and the people here lived in relative poverty. There were two or three tea huts made from old wood, but no food for my Western tummy was available. I felt very blessed. I would be able to buy drinking water in the small ashram store and, sitting in long rows along with the other ashram visitors and the inmates in the large dining hall, eat three meals of rice and curry every day.

A small tin shed in the front of the temple served as the bookstore where photos were also sold. A picture of Amma's feet placed on a yellow cloth with some mysterious script under it caught my attention. I was drawn to it and, before I knew it, I had bought the picture. I placed it in my journal and wrote:

Fishermen at the shore, today Amma's Amritapuri beach

"I am here, where God has placed Her feet on the earth."

Then I fell asleep on a mat on the bottom level of the bunk bed.

The next day I saw Amma. I sat along with many Indians and a few Westerners on the floor of the darshan hut. Pictures of saints and gods were displayed on the walls made of wood and thatch. An intense vibration was in the air. All thoughts were focused on Amma and on the small door through which she would enter the hut at any minute. Amma's seat was prepared at the front of the room. It was a wide Indian-style cot, covered with cloth in a traditional Indian pattern.

Our long meditative wait ended suddenly as the precious door opened almost silently and Amma glided into the room. Her entrance caused a pulsing current of life to circle the formerly quiet room. People stretched their necks and all eyes were focused on one single point: on Amma, who had already placed the nearest person's head on her lap and was running her right hand in long caressing movements over his back.

A woman began to sing, accompanied by the harmonium, and we repeated each verse after her. Sometimes Amma, too, joined in the singing as she cradled and softly, rhythmically rocked the person in her arms. I never thought that one day I, too, would be one of the women who would sing to Amma in the hut, in praise of the Divine, in that heavenly atmosphere.

Waiting for Amma inside the darshan hut

The songs, the Indian heat, the people waiting patiently, and Amma, so near to me, all made me forget time and space. When I, too, was finally in Amma's arms, my mind went silent and made way for pure joy to enter. Amma cradled me in her arms and played with my shawl. I knew she did this for the sole purpose of allowing me to bask in her presence and melt in her embrace.

Feeling full and complete, I left the hut and sat on the sand by the water near the end of the hut where Amma sat. Only the wall of the simple hut separated us. With my eyes closed I let Amma's touch work on me. Pulsating energy flowed through me. My mind was empty, and I could feel all my loved ones were there with me, in my heart. They had all been hugged along with me and blessed by the endlessly flowing river of Love that is Amma!

I am the source
from which you drink.
You cannot possess me;
but become one with me.

Prabha

View from Amritapuri over the backwaters

43

7

FIRST DAYS AT THE ASHRAM

Be the power of Awareness in me, Amma,
So I may know, when Kali's sword cleaves me,
It is you, changing me into Love.

Prabha

Morning Archana in the Kali Temple

Someone once asked me: "Tell me, what has changed in you
since you met Amma?" My answer was spontaneous and simple.
"Amma showed me that I am loved!"

The irrefutable, undeniable fact of being loved and feeling
loved was my first great gift from Amma, and it changed my
entire life. Amma's Love opened up a peaceful space inside of me.
From the vantage point of this space, the space of a loved one, I

45

could view things with a certain detachment and distance. Thus I came to realize how much my life was influenced by the external world. My ego, my entire being, used to react instantly to everything that I encountered. It felt attacked, defended itself, did not want to commit any mistakes, and always wanted to look good; it wanted power. I found myself deeply entrenched in a prison of my own making. Amma's only intention now was to free me from this prison, step by step.

In Amritapuri everything seemed designed to challenge my ego – and not just my ego. Amma intends to confront the ego of everyone who lives there, and I must confess, she could not have found a better place to do so. There I was, in the midst of people who spoke a language that I neither understood nor read. As a result, I could not resort to any clever talk or manipulation to show myself at an advantage, and had to define myself anew, from scratch. The Indian mentality was totally foreign to me, and therefore even manners and respectability seemed to wear a different face there. I unknowingly disregarded or broke so many unknown customs and rules. I was constantly rebuked or set right. As a result, my self-image was pretty battered and beaten up within the first week. Many of my habits drew disapproving headshakes, and nothing that I had learned seemed to work. As a result, I was mercilessly forced to watch my reactions and myself and to learn from them. Many negativities that had cleverly found a hidden existence in me slowly came to light, came out into the open.

Anger and impatience reared their ugly heads, followed by a sense of superiority. I recognized that I expected the ashram residents to live up to my high and holy standards, something that I had thought up in my own head. Because I felt they did not understand or accept me, I started projecting all kinds of shameful things onto others.

I did not think losing my ego would be like this. It was often quite terrible and shameful to see the negative aspects of my personality and to accept them. Amma laid her finger in a skillful manner on my weaknesses. But I stayed on and did not run away.

This was possible only through Amma's pure Love and boundless Compassion. Because of this Love and Compassion, I was connected to her on a very deep level. She touched in me what I had been searching for my entire life.

"This ashram is like a large rock tumbler," Amma often said. "Many rough gems are washed, rinsed, and tumbled in it. They rub against each other till their rough edges and angles are worn down and they begin to shine." Without a doubt I was a very hard gemstone! Along with many magical moments I had in Amma's Presence, I, too, was being put through the polishing cycle in this machine!

In Switzerland my job involved making different kinds of bamboo flutes. I also enjoyed playing these flutes, and had brought some of them with me to India. 'One never knows,' I thought to myself. 'Amma might like to hear my music. Why, she might even ask me to play her something, and I might perhaps even join the group of her musicians!'

But this was not to be. My selfless service, or *seva*, began in the morning at 7am right after the *archana* (the recitation of the 108 names of Amma and the 1000 names of the Divine Mother).

Cutting vegetables for toren

47

I used to cut vegetables for curry and sambar, and this seva held a lot of surprises for me. About a dozen Indians and westerners sat down together on the floor of the large dining hall. In front of us lay cutting boards and large Indian-style knives, which we used to cut mountains of vegetables.

We were managed by an older ashram resident, who was respectfully called *Acchan* (Father), like all other older male Indian residents. Because he was from Calicut, he was called Calicut Acchan. He knew exactly how each vegetable was to be cut, and cut a sample piece for us, which we had to follow. For curry the pieces had to be rectangular, sometimes small, and sometimes large. For *avial*, we had to cut them long, some of them thin, others thick. For *toren*, the vegetables were cut really fine.

It was fascinating to work with these vegetables that I had never seen before. For example, there was a large brown root vegetable called *chena*, or elephant's foot. It was really ugly and we had to oil our hands before touching it. I cut it first in two, and was surprised to see that the inside was a beautiful brilliant color, like a sunset. I realized that human beings can also be like this – difficult on the outside, and beautiful on the inside! In my heart I heard Amma's voice say: "Never speak ill of others. You do not know what they are like on the inside."

On the very first day I learned my first lesson about YOURS and MINE. I busily peeled MY carrots fast so I could later cut them. Actually, I really exerted myself since I wanted to be the fastest carrot peeler in the group! I glanced at the large pile of MY carrots, compared it with those of the others, and was satisfied. I was way out in front in this vegetable cutting competition my mind had thought up. Suddenly I was horrified to see that all MY carrots had vanished! "Who took my carrots?" I thought angrily, and looked around surreptitiously. Ah, it was the young Indian woman sitting next to me. She was busy cutting MY carrots, her dexterous hands wielding the knife fast. Upset, I looked around to see if anyone had seen this mischief. Only then did I notice that some of us, like myself, were peeling the carrots and others, like the young Indian woman, were cutting them. Thanks to this episode, I saw how quickly my mind had turned a harmless, neutral thing like carrots into MINE and YOURS. Simultaneously, I also learned about the standard Indian way of working, where much less ego is involved than in our Western way.

On this day I came face to face with my inherent competitiveness. I recognized how certain attitudes had crept into my life and how I danced to their tunes: Be good so that you can be loved; be fast so that you can be praised; be nice so that people will like you!

Around Amma other values are important: Be fully present in the here and now; focus your full attention on what you are doing; do not think about the fruits of your labor. These would have been the teachings that Amma would have given, which I should have followed while doing my seva.

Often I would retreat to one of the rooms still under construction on the fifth floor of the temple, and play on my favorite flute. I had made this particular flute really well. At home when I improvised on it, my cat would come close to me, rub herself against my leg and arch her back to the music. I had still not relinquished my desire to be discovered as a gifted flautist by Amma. While playing I imagined how Amma was listening to

Helping hand

my music in her room. I was again on an ego trip and wanted her to listen to my wondrous musical skills. In fact, I even wanted her to acknowledge that my music reminded her of the tunes from none other than Lord Sri Krishna's flute! Naturally she would think of me, the virtuoso. She would then ask: "Who is playing on this magical flute?" I would modestly let her know that I myself had made the flute. Of course, Amma would have called me to her room for this conversation. The story did not come to an end with these egoistic daydreams. No, it had just started.

I met my friend Mira during Amma's North India tour in 1990. I had brought a couple of flutes with me. At the place where we were staying in Calcutta, I would sit and play my flutes, improvising the music as I went along. Mira loved it when I played and would come and listen. At one point she said that she would like to learn to play the flute like that. As I wanted to be a person without ego, I spontaneously said to her that in this case I wanted to give her my favorite flute.

Having said that, I instantly regretted it because I was very attached to that flute. So, I took out another flute, a cheap flute I

Amma's little Krishna's

had bought at a market in India and gave it to Mira, hoping to fool her into thinking that this was my bamboo flute. In the evening Mira took this fake flute to Amma in the temple and gave it to her to be blessed. Amma's eyes rested on the flute for a long time and she lovingly caressed it. Today, looking back, I can see how fully aware she was of my manipulation. Then she suddenly said with a horrified look, loud enough that her words dug into my heart painfully: "Oh, but this is not a bamboo flute!"

It was all over. There were no words to describe my condition. Amma is a Master, and this was my first experience at being caught red-handed by her. With a few words she had exposed my secret and reduced me to a poor, shameful heap of misery!

That I finally gave Mira the flute did not let me off the hook. I still had to experience the ways of Kali. She wanted me to have this insight, and it was not easy! A desolate landscape stretched out before me, and I had to cross this arid desert. There was no escape. I cried through an entire Devi Bhava night. Towards the end I knelt before Amma feeling so down, disgusting and malicious that I barely felt like I could allow Amma to hug me. She however, pulled me quickly into her arms. It felt like Mother Kali herself had taken away my sense of shame, lifted the burden off my shoulders. The syllable "Ma Ma Ma" that she murmured plunged like a sword into my ear. It was as if she wanted to slice through the chains that tied me to my misery. With that, my first lesson in 'ego bashing' came to an end.

The next day I sat for a long time in front of the statue of Kali, who claims the egos of human beings with her sword. I gazed at the severed head in her hand. I thought to myself that that could be my head, which she had sawed off yesterday. I thanked her with my whole heart and prayed for eyes that could see what she was trying to show me. After six months, Mira returned the flute to me. I will always remember this episode with Mira and the flute as a precious teaching from Amma.

Kali at Amritapuri

8

Kali,
Last night you visited me
in the ecstasy of dance·

Your dark form was my body,
Your red dress my attire.
Your power ripped through me
And destroyed all boundaries.
I became earth, I became sky,
I danced with surrender through many lives.

You were fire, Kali, unforgiving.
Laying carefully built gardens to waste,
Promising me new life from the wounds.
You led me to my limits
And I looked at my death.
Skinless, I walked with you
through my fear.

I first thought you are the night in me,
The darkness, the unlived
That awaits salvation.
You showed me
That you are the whole.
Pure, unconditional Love,
That can kill, and resurrect
a life, dancing in God.

Prabha

Boys of Amma's orphanage

9

A Zero Is A Hero

If you want to find peace in the outer world,
Your inner world must be at peace.

Amma

I desperately needed a few days away from the ashram! It was all too much for me. Too uncomfortable, too difficult, too hot, too dusty, too this, too that! I was up to my neck in it, and in such moments running away has always been my *modus operandi*.

I hatched what seemed to me a very clever plot to hide from Amma that I was actually just chickening out. Satisfied with my idea, I entered the hut for darshan and waited patiently, my heart full of hope till it was my turn to be hugged. Then I asked Amma innocently, "Amma, tomorrow two *brahmacharinis* are going to work at the orphanage. Can I accompany them and do something useful there?"

Amma looked deeply into my eyes and asked: "Can you make yourself very small?" "Yes, sure, Amma," I said. I pressed the thumb and forefinger of my right hand together to show her just how small I could make myself. Amma only replied, "Then go." The next day I climbed into the old Ambassador car, squeezed myself into the last corner seat and closed my eyes in anticipation of the hair-raising ride through India's crowded streets.

At the orphanage it turned out I was the orphan! Totally out of my depth, without any language skills, I found myself again on the sidelines. The children, however, were happy and asked me to sing. I consoled myself thinking I was useful after all, and was also a little proud of my musical success. Unfortunately, I soon learned that the children were less interested in my singing than in seeing my gold tooth, which glistened in the sunlight whenever I opened my mouth to sing!

Morning bath in the old orphanage

The brahmacharinis had a lot to do and talk to each other about. The first night I went to bed early. I fell asleep on a thin old straw mat in a tiny room and tried to drown my misery in sleep. The brahmacharinis in the meantime were talking animatedly with each other in the dining room. I woke up when they entered the room. Lights were turned on, and they made themselves comfortable on the mats, cracked open some peanuts and continued eating and chatting.

I lived like that for three days, as the useless one! Actually, looking back, everyone was nice to me. It was the language barrier and differences in culture that made me feel like an inept hanger-on. Slowly it dawned on me what Amma had meant about making myself small. My ego was in no way prepared for such a pruning, and my brilliant idea of taking a holiday from the ashram turned out to be a super flop!

On the third night a truck driver from the ashram stopped at the orphanage to eat something and recover from driving in the torrential rains. I packed my meager belongings and quickly went back to the ashram with him. Because of the rainwater, our drive back was more like a cruise than a truck ride. The driver skillfully steered the vehicle without incident up to the backwaters near the ashram. At three in the morning we woke the boatman to ferry us across the swiftly flowing water, which had risen high up

Bhajans in the sand

the embankment. In the darkness the currents pulled at our boat, and both men had to struggle and help each other to row the boat and anchor it at the jetty near the ashram. I sneaked through the stillness of the temple to my bed. In the orphanage I had learned a lesson, one of Amma's teachings. A zero is a hero. Make your ego a zero, and become a hero. Amma never said anything to me about my excursion to the orphanage, but I think I failed that test, too! The next morning dawned with clear bright blue skies. The severe rain had transformed the backwaters. The shores were clean, strewn with small islands of sand and stone formed by the water. Lagoon-like pools of water filled the riverbed. Amma was calling for a swim! The announcement spread like lightening in the temple. Only women allowed. I ran over the sands, past the coconut palms, and reached the water. Amma was already there along with a dozen Western women. They had all removed their saris and tied the underskirt around their chest. That was what the precursor to our current Amritapuri swimsuit. I did the same and saw that Amma was swimming and playing with a few women in the middle of the backwaters. A delightful frivolity was in the air, and our happy laughter echoed over the water like a prayer of gratitude to Mother Nature, who had gifted us this rare opportunity to swim with Amma.

I took this happy scene deep inside. In its joy all the feelings of inadequacy I had had at the orphanage paled and vanished. I realized with wonder that the salty waters of the backwaters were now mixed with the sweet rainwaters from the previous night's torrential downpour. I happily stood on a sandbank and watched the swimmers around Amma. Up above in the blue sky, eagles flew in dreamy circles and watched us.

Suddenly I became alert, as though jolted into awareness by some strong force. I turned my attention to Amma. She stood in the middle of the water on firm ground. Her gaze burned through the distance separating us and reached me. It was as if she had turned on an alarm in me. At that very moment I saw someone near me sinking into the water. Without thinking I dove in, grabbed hold of an arm, then a human form, and dragged it to the surface. In the blink of an eye Amma was with us, and took into her arms the small Japanese lady I had pulled out of the water. I only realized much later, when I read this lady's story in *Matruvani*, the ashram's publication, that I had been Amma's instrument in saving a life.

Dancing with the orphans

10

A NAME FROM AMMA

One is tempted to say:
"You have lost everything!"
But is it not what really matters?
Losing everything to gain everything?

Prabha

After spending four months at the ashram, it was time for me to leave. The time with Amma had changed my life. At home I used to teach courses in self-discovery by playing on sacred instruments and singing. I had put these courses together myself and was in the process of creating an advanced course. After meeting Amma my desire to do this work vanished into thin air. The only thing that I wanted was to be taken under Amma's wing, to live and grow under her care in her ashram in India. I felt I had found the right way for my life. Amma was my Master. The chance to live in the ashram in India, where life in the old days around 1990 was not so easy, was the perfect opportunity to work on myself and discover the mystery in my heart.

My deep connection to Amma helped me take this leap away from the security of my life in Switzerland, my work, and above all my two adult daughters whom I loved above everything else. I had the unshakeable faith that I had found the right path and knew with certainty that everyone I loved would be taken care of. I trusted the divine energy that was weaving itself in and around me. However, instead of simply being thankful and happy about this wonderful development in my life, I wanted more. And this more was a spiritual name from Amma. I discovered that a few female ashramites from the West had received this gift, and I thought that a personal name from Amma would deepen my relationship with her. Well, at least it would build a hotline to Amma between India and Switzerland.

"Later," Amma said to me when I expressed my desire to her. She must have sensed my many crazy expectations dancing in the air in front of her eyes! I had been christened Anna Elizabeth and my parents used to call me Annelies. At the age of 36, I had wanted to be called by my real first name, Anna. For me the two syllables in this name connected me to the earth element and represented a strong bond with Mother Earth. Imagine: I even wanted Amma to bear this in mind when she would give me a name! No way did I want a name like Amritapriya, Rema Devi or Ishwari. I wanted something short, preferably with two A's. I was so ignorant and brazen in making my request that Amma gave me another five months to think about the meaning of the word surrender. Finally, half a year later, at the end of a Devi Bhava night as I knelt before Amma to receive my name, I told Ramakrishna Swami that I was prepared to accept any name that Amma would choose for me.

Amma looked at me for a long time and I smiled back at her. Then she pulled me to her and whispered in my ear: "Frafee, Frafee, Frafee." The sound of these words still echoed in my ears as Amma got up, walked to the edge of the stage and blessed everyone with a shower of flower petals to the rising crescendo of music from the swamis. Behind the curtains at the side, Swami Ramakrishna asked me: "And what is your name?" "It is Frafee" I said, still dazed, and could hear him laugh. Then he said: "You are Prabha, the effulgence of Divine Light. It sounds like Frafee when spoken in the dialect of the fisher folk here in Parayakadavu."

"Prabha." She had named me "Prabha," with an emphasis on the last "a." Amma had heard my prayers, fulfilled my wishes and made me happy with a short name with two vowels, both even A's. I gave as much value to this name as if I had just received a professorship at a university or initiation into priesthood. What I did not realize in my joyful delirium was that it would be a full year before Amma called me by this name.

My expectations were very much alive. My Indian name brought out the pride in me, and rather than reflecting on its inner meaning, I mistakenly thought it would create a deeper bond to my Amma family. I let hours and days go by without tuning in to the effulgence of divine light that my name should have evoked in me. Amma gave me time, a lot of time, to integrate the divine light, *prabha*, into my life. For months she let me have various experiences of the unending expectations of my mind, which thought out various scenarios, wishes and dreams. During this entire period of learning and suffering I remained nameless. When Amma addressed me it was always with a YOU, or she pointed to me, or looked at me.

At that time there were only a few ashram residents, and whenever Amma took the boat across the backwaters to go for a house visit or a program nearby we stood at the jetty to bid her farewell. I am reminded of one such day. The simple boat was tied to the ashram jetty and the boatman was waiting for Amma. Those traveling with her had already got into the little bus parked on the other shore. Those of us staying behind lined Amma's path, standing in a row in the sand under the palm trees. We could see Amma approaching from afar. Of course, we recognized her instantly. Only she walked like this, filled with a tremendous power, so bound to the earth and yet hardly touching it. She smiled at us, pulled each one of us close to her, breathed in through her nose making this wonderfully close, intimate sound that was a goodbye kiss for us. That day she stood in front of us Westerners, looked at us closely and said our names out loudly.

My expectations shot up sky high! Now, now was the moment it would happen. Oh, my God! Today was the day. As she reached me, Amma glanced at me briefly and moved on to the next person, calling her by name. I simply stood there, the wind literally knocked out of me. Breathless, I stood there and watched her get into the boat, stand in it and let herself be ferried across the

Departure to a program in Trivandrum

water, the living image of a Goddess who is one with the elements. Looking back, I hope a large portion of my ego also departed along with her over the water to a new shore.

I stood there hurt and discouraged. I was now her nameless child ready to relinquish the fairy tales I had woven around my name. I once more felt called to merge with the meaning of my name, with the effulgent light I really was in the mask of a form. Why could I not let go of these thoughts connected to my name? Why could I not simply be a witness to my thoughts and move forward towards what I really was? It took many more painful moments and months before I could integrate my inner self, that space of light and love, which had been covered by my upbringing and conditioning.

One year later I found myself on the Europe tour with Amma. I had been in Switzerland earlier to sell and get rid of my possessions. My daughters kept the apartment with its furnishings; the books were shipped to the ashram library; and my personal belongings were packed in an old trunk used for overseas travel. I was now ready for a possession-free ashram life. I then wrote Amma a letter, which I never mailed. It went as follows:

> *Dear Amma,*
> *I am moving to the ashram even though you may never call me by my name. You may have even forgotten what name you gave me on a Devi Bhava night. I shall think of my namelessness not as humiliation or rejection. This is not going to stop me from being together with you in India.*

Before I left, I tore up the letter and boarded the train for Zurich where Amma was holding a program. On the third morning I knelt before her and helped people into her lap. There were only a few people left in line when I suddenly heard the word 'Prabha.' It was so sudden and unexpected that I did not know whether I

heard it or imagined it. I continued to work and heard it yet again for the second time. I took a quick look at Amma. Did she say it? No, not possible. She was holding the last visitor in a close embrace.

After this she called me for darshan. "Prabha" she whispered in my ear, "Prabha." All my stories about my name dissolved, and a liberating laughter found its way from deep within me onto my face. Surprised, I looked at Amma, who was repeatedly whispering my name.

Her voice grew louder, and her hands drew a large effulgence of light above my head in the air. The people in the hall listened, laughed and enjoyed the scene. Finally, Amma held me in front of her as if I were a little child, and called out repeatedly, "Prabhaprabhaprabhaprabha," simultaneously shaking me as if I were her small baby and she my mother playing with me.

Later, with a smile on my face as I cleaned the hall, the realization dawned on me that Amma had been playing a game with me the whole time. Weeks, months and years long she had played this hide-and-seek game with me. She did this as long as it took me to become aware of the lessons she was trying to teach. My love and attention should be directed towards the goal, to live connected to the whole, and not towards getting possibly the best name from Amma. This 'name game' helped me to grow in awareness. Even today I am reminded of Amma's words: "

> *Connect with the Divine every day, and let this be the most important thing you do that day."*

Devotees decorated Amma as Radha

11

Divine Mother,
The Earth – your Lap
The starry Skies – your Garment
The Wind – your Breath
Fire consumes my heart.

Star Mother
You show my night
Your moon shines brightly on my wounds
My lonely cry
Echoes in the Dark

Sun Mother
Come! Transform my desert
Into a lush blossoming field
Let me bake bread
With the grains of your Love!

Prabha

12

THE COOK

Come, show me the pattern of your yarn.
I want to knit the gown of liberation.
And show me how to cross
a wall of thorns without armor.

Prabha

One day, I was promoted from the seva of cutting vegetables to being a cook. My kitchen was located in the sand of a courtyard behind the small temple and was an excellent place to practice jumping over the hurdles one faces in spiritual life.

Kitchen yard in the olden days

I was focused on being a 'self-made woman,' but actually only appeared to be so. Amma's *sankalpa*, her strong intention, was a loving support that flowed one hundred percent into my cooking skills and allowed me to cook as she would have wanted me to, without wasting anything.

Thanks to her, my soups were edible every time I made them, and while they were created out of whatever ingredients I had at hand that day, I learned many lessons, and experienced beautiful and desperate moments. This seva shrunk my ego and transformed it.

Cooking on a North India tour

In the beginning of my career I cooked a soup for seventeen Western ashram guests, twice a week. The fine, healthy dinner was available on the gallery of the Kali temple, after the community had joined in bhajan. I dare say that soup was the predecessor to the many specialties offered at the Western Café today.

I bravely built my cooking stove every Tuesday and Friday on the sandy ground of the courtyard, knowing fully well that the next time I would need it, it would have vanished as if removed by a magical hand. I never investigated this 'magic,' but rather I would build a new stove every time, hoping in my heart for success and saying a prayer for equanimity while digging a round hole in the ground, and placing three bricks in a circle around the edge. The tureen-like cooking vessel would then be placed on top of these bricks and a fire was lit under it.

I had a free hand in choosing the vegetables and loved this creative seva that was always full of hidden surprises. Often I would even go right after lunch to the kitchen shelves and look for things I could use for the evening soup. My work earned me the compliments of the guests, but not the help of the Indian cooks and I often found myself wishing they would teach me. Since they rarely did, I had to learn to be independent.

I love making a fire and knew the various woods used for this back home, but was clueless about how to use coconut palm

My kitchen

fronds and such other Indian wood as I had at my disposal. Some wood burnt quickly. Huge flames would dance around my cooking pot and my heart would beat faster with anticipation. But soon I found that though this fire was impressive, it did not generate any heat. Other wood looked usable but, despite all attempts on my part, I could not get it to burn. So I had to take a chance every time. I worked hard finding and cutting the right wood. I moved it around strategically in the stove, hoping fervently that it would burn. Fortunately, most of the time the fire did burn, and with the help of my flashlight, I could see the soup bubbling in my cooking pot.

Often the darkness spread over my kitchen as I worked. Bhajans echoed over the distance from the temple and Amma's voice found its way to me. She warmed my heart and gave me the strength to carry on shining my flashlight deep into the cooking pot to check on the soup and connecting myself to the vast space within me that helped me with the gift of patience.

I liked my seva because it was full of adventure and reminded me of fairy tales I had read as a child. Fairy tales were my all-time favorites and I read and reread in them about the highs and lows of life, and was fascinated by the various trials and tribulations the characters had to go through. The moral of the story was always the victory of good over evil, and even then, as a grown woman, I must have identified with this truth. I perceived myself as a cook, who had to triumph over the various trials until she would discover the diamond within her heart. I had no doubt that Amma was fully aware of my experiences, in fact even orchestrated them, and I made sure I nurtured a close connection with her inside of me.

Occasionally, Amma appeared unannounced on the balcony of the Kali temple where the soup was served. She sat down with the group of diners, accepted few spoons of soup on a steel plate, tasted it and gave me feedback about how not to waste anything, to create as little garbage as possible, and to use salt sparingly because it was bad for health. It was pure joy to experience Amma so close, and in such a friendly mood.

One evening, Amma disclosed that in the near future I would be cooking for over a hundred people. I sat next to her and smiled, embarrassed and a little disbelieving. In my mind I could see myself crouched in front of a gigantic fire, and peering into an enormous cooking pot with my little flashlight.

I did not guess at the time that Amma was planning to construct a new kitchen and that I would soon be standing at an artistically constructed fireplace, making breakfast and dinner for many guests who came from the West, and serving it in an improvised café.

Well, back to my kitchen in the courtyard, and the Indian women whom I liked despite our differences. They gave me the feeling of being a little integrated into this unknown culture. Slowly, through our work, a sense of friendly community grew among us that transcended cultural differences. As a result of this, I learned how to get a fire going using the various parts of coconut palm. The good wood was freed from its hiding place, and while working, my Indian sisters taught me the most important Malayalam words used in the kitchen.

I now felt accepted into the circle of our Indian kitchen. There were precious moments when I felt like I now belonged to our kitchen team and was accepted and integrated.

Such thoughts fed my desire to be liked and to be popular. Even as a child I had learned from my grandmother the importance of being well-liked, and in our family this was a basic requirement in life. It led me to confuse being liked with being loved. For me, being liked became the main goal worth striving for in life, probably because I had no real experience of being loved.

To show me very clearly that being popular was based on a very shaky, fragile foundation that could be manipulated by outside forces and collapse at any time, Amma initiated a special story for me.

I had received instructions to bring the unsold leftover soup to the dining hall, where the brahmacharis (monks) ate their simple meals. There it turned into a dessert of sorts for whoever was present, and everyone loved my soup. The young men were glad to have a change from *kanji*, the rice soup they ate for dinner every night, and I often received compliments and flattery. My popularity barometer was rising from day to day and seduced me into doing something dishonest.

One day I decided to put a couple of extra deciliters of soup to cook on the fire, and naturally after dinner, just as I had hoped, there was some soup left over. I happily took this 'leftover' I had made on purpose and entered the monks' dining hall. Today I had something delicious to offer and they would reward me with praise and attention, I thought to myself.

Unfortunately, all my plans came to nothing. Amma was waiting for me in the hall. She stood in the middle of the room appearing larger than life and watched me as I stood there, my deception and manipulation fully exposed. Sort of like the statue of the judge on the portal of the cathedral in my hometown, she was looking down at me, stretching her hands out towards my soup tureen. She took it from me and inspected its contents. Then she asked for the ladle, which in those days was made from a coconut shell and distributed the soup among those present like a loving mother. Joy spread on everyone's faces. Not just because of the culinary treat, but mainly because of the person serving it. While everyone enjoyed the soup, Amma returned the empty soup tureen to me. Quietly, without letting the others hear a word, Amma impressed upon me that my duty was to cook only for the Western visitors, and that I should prepare just enough soup to feed them. No leftovers ever. I slunk away, having been caught red-handed.

It was only much later, after many eye-opening experiences, that the desire to be liked was extinguished. I learned how fragile popularity can be. One action, sometimes even a single word, can destroy it. Anyone who builds on this foundation will never get any peace.

Only when true Love is present is a real exchange and true closeness possible between beings. Only through the inspiration of this Love can an authentic meeting take place. True love is the energy in whose light difficulties, arguments, misunderstandings and failures can be brought out and transformed. This Love radiates constantly from Amma, and in its light our heart begins to grow and opens up like a beautiful flower, touched by the warm and soothing rays of the morning sun.

13

The tale of the bamboo tree

During my time as a bamboo flute maker, I often felt the desire to become a flute myself, to become a hollow tube through which God's song could be sung to the world. However, only after reading this fairy tale did I realize my lack of awareness of the pain involved on this journey from being time-bound to beyond time. I had suppressed this pain and deceived myself by only looking at the fairytale-like, magical aspects of this growth process. Now wiser and more aware, I feel quiet tears of gratitude and pain stream down my cheeks. I would like to share an abridged version of this story with you, and I must confess it is not really a fairy tale at all.

Once upon a time there was a beautiful garden right in the middle of planet earth. The Mother of the Universe loved to go for a walk there. A noble bamboo tree was her favorite out of all the bushes and trees in the garden. Year after year this bamboo tree grew into a stunning beauty, growing taller and more graceful. One day, the Divine Mother thoughtfully approached her bamboo, which bowed deeply in great reverence. The Divine Mother hugged the bamboo and said: "My beloved Bamboo, I need you."

It appeared that the day of all days had come, the day for which the bamboo had been created. The tree answered softly: "Mother, I am ready, use me according to your will."

"Bamboo," spoke the Divine Mother, "To use you, I have to first cut you."

"Cut me? Me, whom you have made the most beautiful in the garden? No, please, please no. Use me in whichever way it pleases you, but do not cut me."

"My dear Bamboo, if I do not cut you, then I cannot use you," said the Divine Mother seriously.

In the garden everything suddenly fell deathly still. The wind held its breath. Slowly the bamboo bent down and whispered: "Mother, if you cannot use me without cutting me, then… cut me."

"My dear Bamboo, I must also remove all your leaves and branches."

"Oh no, please do not destroy my beauty, please at least spare my leaves and branches," pleaded the tree.

The Mother replied, "Bamboo, if I do not cut them also, I cannot use you."

The sun hid its face. A butterfly fled fearfully from the scene. The bamboo, trembling with dread of what was to come, said slowly, "Mother, cut them off."

"My dear Bamboo, I must do one more thing. If I do not cut your stem in two, I cannot use you."

This time the bamboo bowed down quietly to the earth, acquiesced and said,

"Please cut me in two."

The Divine Mother began to remove the bamboo leaves and branches. She cut it in two, reaching into the very core. She carried the bamboo lovingly in her arms to a spring where fresh sparkling water gushed forth. There she laid the bamboo carefully on the ground, attached its one end to the spring and positioned the other end on the adjacent field, where the crop was thirsting for water. The spring sang a song of welcome to the bamboo and the clear, glittering water shot happily through the canal, which the body of the bamboo had now become, onto the dry fields. They had been waiting for water for such a long time!

So the bamboo became a great blessing. When it was tall and beautiful, it grew only for itself. But as it bowed down, it became the instrument of the Divine Mother, who used it to make her land fertile.

Afternoon on the North Indian tour

14

SEVA AND SAMADHI

You,
evening wind that caresses the palms,
you whisper tenderly amidst the quivering leaves.
Your unseen hand leads the birds home to their nests
and drops the curtain of night over the world.
I watch this and am alone.
Do you know I long for your touch?
You sing in my heart, but I hear you not.
How can I dance when your Love is far away?
Do you see me when you walk by without even a glance?
The hem of your dress kisses the earth.
Let me be a drop of water that you drink,
a grain of sand under your feet.

Prabha

There hangs in the Kali Temple even today a large cast iron bell whose strident tones echo throughout the ashram shortly before Amma comes for darshan, before a class starts and during the singing of the *arati*. The bell also rings to summon everyone for morning archana.

It has replaced the monk whose duty it was to wake us up at four thirty every morning, knocking on each door and waking everyone up with a loud 'Namah Shivaya.'

My first encounter with this temple bell was on the first night of my stay at Amritapuri. It rang around midnight, jolting me out of a deep slumber. I opened the door of my room on the gallery of the temple and peeped over the metal railing into the hall.

"Amma is calling for brick seva," I heard a male voice call out. Leaning out over the railing, I could see the owner of this voice, a figure in a white dhoti, disappear through the rear entrance of the temple, presumably to wake up others.

I had to hold onto the cool white metal of the railing for a few minutes to orient myself and be fully awake. I stroked my finger lightly along the artistic wrought iron balustrade and remembered my dream from that night. The setting for this dream was right there on that railing. In my dream I lay on my back on the railing with Amma standing at my side. She had positioned me in such a way that my entire spine rested on the metal bar. Standing next to me she pressed lightly with her forefinger on my perfectly

Tuesday in the Kali Temple, Amma is sitting on the right side.

balanced body. I began to slowly lean towards the red floor of the balcony. When she reduced the pressure of her finger my body shifted back to its original position. She again exerted pressure and this time I leaned towards the floor of the temple several feet below. Every time I was in danger of crashing either onto the balcony or temple floor, she brought me back to balance in the middle by simply reducing or increasing the pressure of her finger on my body. The intense surrender and unshakeable faith I showed in Amma in that dream stays vividly with me even to this day. I lay in her hands without the slightest trace of fear. My surrender was total! This would not have been possible in the waking state.

Back in the present, I followed the call for brick seva and exited the temple through the same door as the monk. My glance fell on Amma's small courtyard, a square piece of sandy land bordered on two sides with decorative bricks. These bricks had been removed from one side and a short plank of wood formed a makeshift bridge over a narrow strip of water. On the other side of this in the middle of the coconut grove stood several people in a long, long row, working silently to pass the bricks needed for building the temple from one hand to the other. This row of tireless workers stretched from the street along the ocean through the coconut grove right up to the Kali Temple. Visitors and villagers worked alongside the ashramites, forming a long human chain. Next to me stood Amma, who worked just like everyone else. She was directing the entire operation and worked powerfully, allowing the bricks to pass quickly through her hands to the next person, giving them a quick darshan!

Feeling drunk with sleep, I could think of nothing else other than just standing next to Amma. She let me pass her the bricks, initiating me into my first encounter with night seva at the ashram. The air was cool, the ocean waves thundered on the beach, and the night sky was dotted with a million stars that twinkled at us between the palm trees.

I was in paradise. Passing one brick after the other to Amma, I completely lost body consciousness and awareness of any physical limitations. It was only when I almost fell off the narrow plank of wood into the water on my way back to my brick seva from

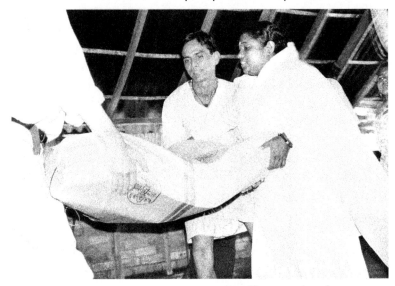

Paper arrives for our press

an errand Amma sent me on, that I became aware of my fatigue. "*Aiyo!* You sit," said Amma, leading me by the hand to sit under a palm tree. I sat down and watched Amma at work. It was fascinating. I had the most desirable seat in the universe and could watch the tiny white form of the Divine Mother as she deftly passed bricks to the person next to her. It was clear that each one of her movements, which were so perfect, arose from an invisible source, from beyond. I could hear her laugh, give directions, admonish the sevites to be careful and to concentrate. She did all this with blissful joy streaming out from every pore. A powerful vibration emanated from her and spread out over everyone present. It transformed our actions from mere work into the sanctified service of helping construct Amma's temple.

After our work was over we all sat down in the small courtyard. Amma gave everyone banana chips from a large bowl and later also a small cup of coffee. But I missed the coffee. Sitting on the warm sand, I had fallen into a blissful, dreamless sleep with my head resting on my chest.

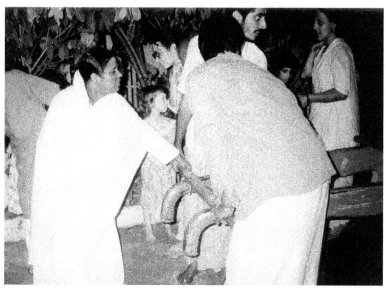

From then on I was always there when the bell rang for the night time brick seva. I loved walking quietly and with awareness, carrying bricks through the coconut palm grove. Reciting my mantra while working filled me with a beautiful lightness and I learned how to use my energy with full concentration.

One special night after we had worked for a long time, Amma invited us to her courtyard, which also doubled as her garden. The sky was studded with stars and a cool wind from the sea caressed my hair. Amma sat on a cot in the middle of the courtyard, laughing and playing with her pillow. She shook it, threw it in the air, stuck her hands out and caught it. Sometimes she set the pillow on her head like a little child. Then Amma sang. She sang not only for all of us but also for the moon, the stars and all creatures on earth. The night wind carried her voice into the universe and deep into my heart.

After singing a song that expressed an intense poignant longing for God, Amma went into *samadhi*. Everything around was stillness and peace. We knew that we should leave then, silently and without touching Amma. Like the others, I also stood up and wanted to leave, but as I quickly glanced at Amma I saw a beam of light emanating from her. Its brilliance drew a glowing line on the sand, which ended where I was standing and touched my foot. An incredible power possessed my body. Its energy made me fall down on my knees and bow down deep. Amma sat motionless. Her tiny foot rested on the edge of her bed. Slowly and gently this power lifted my torso and laid my head delicately on Amma's feet. By now I had given up control over my body, but my senses were fully awake. I experienced a surge of incredible Love as my lips tenderly kissed Amma's feet. My life became timeless. This same power made me bow down once again and put me back on my feet. Like in a dream I observed Amma's motionless figure as she sat still. The beam of light had disappeared. I slowly left the courtyard and walked through the temple back to my room.

That night I could not sleep. A painful longing filled my entire being. Seeking relief, I wandered early in the morning into the kitchen and began cutting vegetables hoping the work would ground me and help me process the events of the last night. However, the very opposite happened. My longing only increased and drove me to wander restlessly around the ashram.

Amma was giving darshan in the hut. It was a Devi Bhava day, and we residents were supposed to stay in the background and make room for the visitors. I sought out the backwaters on the other end of the ashram to find some inner peace, but even that did nothing to help my pitiable condition. All at once I could feel Amma calling me. I hurried to the darshan hut. I was sure that Amma wanted to see me, and entered the hut confidently making my way through the dense crowd of visitors. When Amma spotted me she waved me to her side and laid my head on her lap. I had come home, to that place where my inner emotional chaos could end. Later Amma asked me to fan her with a hand-held fan made of palm leaves. I stood for hours behind her cot and closely watched hundreds of Indian faces as they came up to Amma. As

View from the front steps of the Kali Temple

I did so, a tremendous feeling of mental peace came over me, and along with it immense feelings of love and compassion for everyone. I saw how the faces of the people coming for Amma's darshan reflected the human condition, revealing sorrow, joy, confusion and a myriad of other emotions. Their faces were weathered and marked by life as they came into Amma's arms for help, seeking her motherly love and embrace. But after a while, my old way of thinking returned. In fact, this was another blessing because I was, perhaps for the first time, aware of how my While standing behind Amma, I got the chance to observe how my awareness was slowly changing. I could see how my normal awareness with all its personal judgments and opinions pulls me away from the natural state of love. Regardless, the pendulum of my mind had me in its grip again. It swung from clear to cloudy, sunshine to rain, happiness to sorrow. It moved from fulfillment to need, from the past to the present. It fluctuated like this for hours, for days – and continues to do so even now. Once in a while it stops to make room for those glorious moments when I can escape its grip and dive into timelessness.

15

THE BACKPACK

No large bag for the road
Just a little sack,
And then, nothing at all.
In the stillness,
God and God will meet
In my heart.

Prabha

Entrance to my hut

I sat waiting quietly in the darshan hut to get a last hug from Amma before she left for Australia. I intended to stay behind with the brahmacharis and brahmacharinis in the orphaned ashram, knowing that later I would have the privilege of joining Amma's group in Singapore and traveling with her to Reunion and Mauritius.

A melancholy mood prevailed in the twilight inside the darshan hut. No music, no songs! The darkness of night was fast approaching as I knelt and waited for my turn. Gazing at the pictures of the various saints that hung on the walls made of wood and palm leaves, I slowly made my way towards Amma. Soon I was in her arms, said goodbye and received her blessings. Amma looked concerned when I knelt before her after the darshan. She quickly pulled me back into her arms and gave me a second, very long hug.

Afterwards I lay down to sleep on the floor of my hut, which I had just moved into the day before. It did not have any doors as yet and I could see the reflection of the flashlights in the coconut grove, which extended all the way to the street by the sea. There Amma and the swamis were on their way through the sand and trees to the cars that would take them to the airport. I saw the headlights through the palm trees, heard the motor start up, and then they were gone.

I heard the waves roar and thunder as they broke on the shore, saw the lights of countless fireflies blinking in the darkness, and thus fell asleep on the thin mat in my new home. I was the first inhabitant of this rudimentary, traditional building with three rooms made of palm leaves. The entire structure stood on cement pillars. My room was right next to the water.

The following morning, I awoke with a high fever. I was alone. The Indian girls had not yet moved into the two rooms next door since Amma was away and the rooms, which opened out into the sands near the water, had no doors. I slept the entire day, drank some water from my bottle and tried to inform the German doctor who lived with his wife and two small children in the Kali Temple.

Working with Amma

He came into the hut the next day. After observing me in a clinical, detached manner, without even examining me, he thought that I would be okay after a day or two.

I became delirious with a high fever for the next two days. Once in a while someone came by, but left just as quickly, helpless and not knowing what to do. I lay in a stupor, heard spiders and cockroaches rustling through the freshly woven palm leaves that made up the walls of my room. Sometimes I felt a rough tongue licking my legs. Fat rats, as large as Indian cats, were licking my sweat. My room was built on their territory, and because there was no door, they had free access to my sickbed.

Their presence and that of the other guests from the animal kingdom ceased to disturb me. I sank into a pleasant, sleepy, spaced-out state, clearly felt Amma's presence and was bathed in light. The third day when a young woman checked in on me, I heard myself say: "If I do not get any antibiotics now, it will be too late." Well, the doctor came by again and all hell broke loose. Everyone was panicking, except me. I had slowly slipped away from anxiety and pain into a state of no-mind.

I was immediately moved into the empty dormitory on the first floor of the temple and put on medication. A hastily assembled 'nursing staff' gave me water to drink every fifteen minutes. Sometimes, because I protested and made such a fuss, water had to be practically forced down my throat.

Today this would not happen, because our ashram now has a hospital with professional staff and intravenous medication for cases such as mine. But at that time I was not a well-behaved patient and did not want anyone to touch me, nor did I want to drink anything. I refused all offers of help because I wanted to remain in my weightless state and not be disturbed.

Slowly I came out of my delirium. Thoughts started surfacing in my mind, and along with them the past and especially the future. I became aware of having planned to see Amma and immediately turned into a docile, obedient patient whose only goal was the trip to Singapore!

Even though I had become weak and skinny, I gave it my all and was there with the others as the driver held open the door to the small bus which was to take us to the airport. Our departure was delayed by a small problem. One of the American ladies had sprained her foot and was on crutches. She was desperately trying to find someone to carry her overloaded backpack. Despite her asking several people, no one was ready to take on the extra burden in addition to their own luggage. Finally, I stretched my hand out and took the backpack, even though in my condition I was barely able to stand and take care of my own bag. Anyway, that problem was solved and we drove off to the airport, boarded our flight and landed safely in Singapore.

Amma was already sitting in the airplane that was bound for Mauritius and was watching us as we tried to get into the seats near her.

When she saw me, the smile on her face was replaced by a look of concern and she was miming my emaciated body and weak condition.

In the plane

Stunned, she watched as I handed the American woman her backpack and then summoning my very last ounce of strength stowed my own bag in the overhead bin above my seat. In Mauritius this game with the backpacks continued in reverse order. I took both my and the second backpack and staggered, bearing this double load into the lounge, deposited them both in a corner and ran to Amma. She had just started hugging those of us who had joined the tour, and eventually ended up hugging practically the entire ground crew at the airport as well!

As our boarding was announced over the public address system, Amma stood up first. We were all surprised because Amma usually stayed till the very last minute with those devotees who had come to see her off. We watched as she strode purposefully to the corner where I had deposited the American's backpack. She bent down, picked it up, hung it over her shoulder and marched to the gate. Immediately a swarm of helpers hovered around her. Several hands reached for the heavy load on her shoulder. But Amma refused them all and carried the backpack into the plane.

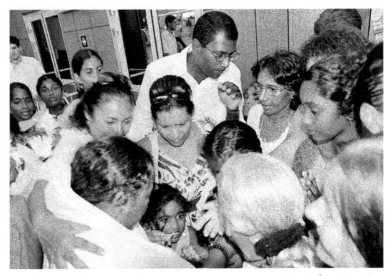

Arrival in Reunion

In this way, she shamed everyone who had been blind and closed to the American woman's need for assistance. In that departure lounge, Amma demonstrated, as always, through her own example rather than through words, that even small ways of helping and serving can have a huge impact. Amma always says we might not always be able to help out financially, but a smile, a loving word, a helping hand, or giving someone your full attention are all things that everyone can do.

At the time when Amma was carrying the backpack I had the feeling that she knew everything about me. That she was closer to me than I wa s to myself, always ready to carry my inner backpack. And I asked myself: "Is she accompanying me on the path I choose to travel, or am I travelling the path that has already been laid out for me? Is she guiding my actions, or watching to make sure I place every step where I am meant to?"

In such moments, I see Amma as the universal life force, eternal awareness living in every facet of my existence, constantly creating new situations to make me grow and move within, towards the very source and foundation of my being.

The inner Mother has no outer qualities. She is silence, absolute consciousness. You cannot even address this silent inner Mother as "Mother" because that is a name. In this highest consciousness, which is the inner Mother, there are no names or forms.

Amma

16

TEA AT MIDNIGHT

In the heart of the labyrinth with thick walls
is shining the gold of your Love
Let me be bliss, for a moment
or for eternity

Prabha

Over the course of the years, the number and kinds of people enjoying the food I prepared grew, and along with this, my collection of cooking pots and responsibilities grew as well. I spent a lot of time in the kitchen. While I worked I watched how ashramites and guests meditated with Amma, did some small unexpected sevas in her presence, or simply accompanied her on a walk across the ashram grounds, full of joy at the prospect of experiencing the kind of delightful *leela* or adventure that happens spontaneously around Amma.

It was often very difficult to know that Amma was out there and I in here in the kitchen, standing in front of my cooking pots. It took a lot of mental control and sense of responsibility not to drop everything and follow Amma. I did my very best to focus on my work. Often during a midnight seva, I slipped away to the kitchen. There I set curds for the next day or soaked some lentils. Thus I soon developed the ability to get by with very little sleep.

One night, it was past midnight actually, after Devi Bhava was over, Swamiji came over to me and said casually, "Be prepared, it is possible that Amma might call you."

I hardly had the time to digest this news in its entirety before a message flew from mouth to mouth through the temple, swiftly like a row of dominoes falling one on top of the other, till it reached me: "Amma is calling Prabha." My heart beat fast as I happily climbed the steps to Amma's room. I entered the small space and saw Amma, who sat on the floor and was playing like a little child with some metal glasses and a water jug. She had created the whole scene just for me, to make me happy. Through this childlike game, in spite of, or maybe because of my lack of Malayalam skills, she wanted to show me how to make a good cup of tea.

I sat down next to her and soon turned without any shyness into an innocent, playing child, as if it were the most natural thing in the world. I was wrapped up in a whole new world born out of that wonderful moment.

Amma filled three glasses full of water, placed them in a row in front of her, and pointing to each of them with her forefinger she counted loudly: "One glass, two glasses, three glasses." Like a child who is deeply immersed, fully absorbed in the game, she commented: "Three cups of water and...," quickly filling another glass from the pitcher, "one cup of milk. Or should we take four cups of water for the tea?" She happily poured the water from the glass with 'milk' back in the pitcher, placed it on the floor, and filled it again with water for the 'tea' "Okay, four glasses," she counted and placed another glass in the row and filled it anew from the water pitcher with 'milk.' "Should we take three glasses of black tea with one glass of milk or four glasses? Hmm, what is better?" she asked.

It was indescribably beautiful to sit next to Amma, the child fully engrossed in the play, fully in the present, and to experience

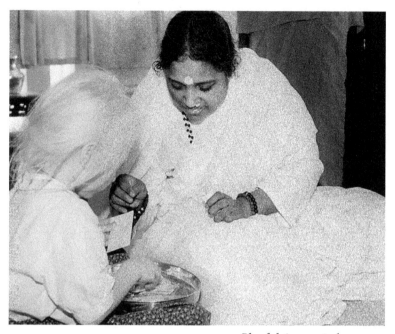

Playful Amma in her room

the transcendent quality and beauty of complete identification with the moment. She showed me, sitting there on the floor of her room, not only how to prepare a good cup of tea, but also the preciousness of a complete action. A perfect action where one is fully present with one's whole being, with all senses, the body and heart. Such action releases an intensely powerful energy, a special grace and a quiet binding love, which touches everyone present. It leads one away from the clichéd ordinary action, towards action that arises from the whole, full of joy and creativity, and free from the ego.

Amma and I were transformed into two children who were happily playing. The five glasses of water became delicious tea, which was now poured into a second pitcher and mixed. Amma held the pitcher high above her head and with effortless dexterity poured tea straight into the glass held low in her other hand. She then laughed and said something to Swamiji who translated for me::

101

"This trick produces a lot of foam and gives the illusion that the glass is completely full. It saves a lot of tea, and brings the tea maker, the *chaiwala*, some easy profit."

With that, the tea lesson came to an end. Amma quickly got up, clapped her hands and happily danced around the room. I followed her rhythm and steps, and we both might have continued to laugh and dance around the room had it not been for a single thought which broke the magic of the moment. Something within me said that Amma must be very busy and doesn't really have time to play this game for long.

It was as if a thick cloud suddenly covered the sun. The unique ambience in the room that was so full of possibilities collapsed and shut down. Amma turned away from me, picked up one of the many letters from devotees that were stacked high on the dresser and began to read.

I took my leave, both happy and sad at the same time. The sorrow of parting sat silently in my heart, which was overflowing with childlike joy. This sorrow, it accompanies me and I know it well. It always visits me at that very time when I try to hold on to something. Its presence shows me that life is a flow and not static. It helps me discover the dynamism of letting go, of moving on and experiencing anew. Let this circle be complete in all of us and let it lead us to discovering a life of fullness.

The inner Mother, whose true nature is infinitude and silence, manifests visibly through this body, so that her children can have a glimpse of the Mother who is deep within.

The reason this external Mother exists is to help you reach the inner Mother, the Mother of the "Mind of Minds."

The inner Mother has none of the external qualities. It is totally silent and attributeless in the "Mind of Minds."

Silence is the language of this inner Mother.

Amma

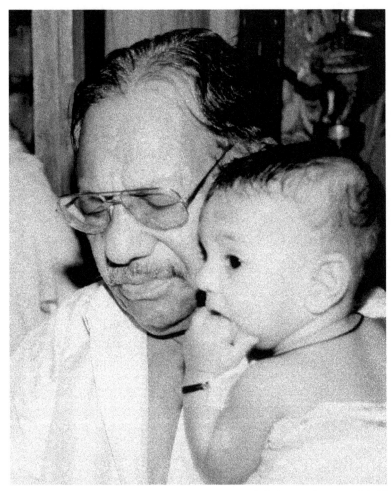

Amma's father with a grandchild

17

THE IDAMANNEL FAMILY

You do not need any new Truth.
All you have to do is to know the Truth that exists
And shines unceasingly in the whole creation.
This Truth is not ancient or modern
But ever the same, immutable and eternally new.

Amma

Kalari 1993

Acchamma, Amma's grandmother

One of the nicest sevas during my early Ashram years began in the wee hours of the morning. Shortly after four I would walk in my freshly washed sari through the darkness of the almost empty ashram and enter the mysterious Kalari, which was where Amma first held Her Krishna and Devi Bhavas.

The spiritually intense atmosphere of this temple always touched me deeply. I was transformed into a servant of God, who reverentially collected the flower garlands and petals from the previous day's *puja*. After this I silently filled a jug with water from the tap near Amma's room and placed it next to the *peetham*, the small wooden stool, in the Kalari. The trident and sword from Amma's early bhava days were placed on this peetham. These and other ritual objects were worshipped and decorated with sandalwood paste and vermillion later in the morning by one of her earliest disciples, today known as Swami Turiyamritananda. While outside on the veranda, the daily fire ceremony, the *homa*, was being conducted. I busied myself inside the temple with cleaning everything and preparing for the rituals of the new day.

At the end I used to sit on the veranda near the fire and wash the brass utensils, working in silence with utmost concentration. I was fascinated to see the *pujari* invoking the auspicious deity Ganesha. Around daybreak, I would also see the form of Amma's grandmother, bent over with age, as she entered the Kalari veranda. This old lady was Amma's father's mother and hence called *Acchamma*. Acchamma came because, even at that advanced age, she and a few helpers would sit down daily and make garlands with the flowers left there by neighbors and devotees, to decorate the pictures and statues of deities in the Kalari.

Before the sun came up I would be on my way around the ashram, the backwaters and in the neighbor's gardens to pick more flowers. During these times, as I walked by Amma's parents' – the Idamannels' – house, I would hear Amma's mother, Damayanti Amma, reciting the 1,000 names of Sri Lalitha, the Divine Mother, in her puja room. A little while later she would already be in front of the house going about her work. Often she

Damayantiamma, Amma's mother

would be pulling large coconut-palm fronds behind her. She worked carefully to weave large panels from them; these were used to build our huts. The stick-like ribs of the palm leaves were used to make brooms, with which the diligent brahmacharinis swept the sandy ashram grounds long before the bell for the first archana in the Kali Temple sounded.

The sandy spot under the palm trees between Amma's parents' house and the backwaters was a shipyard. Under Amma's father's watchful eyes, hired shipbuilders would construct large fishing boats equipped with cabins for his fleet. During my flower-gathering excursions, I watched in wonder as, after mere weeks of work, the builders turned rough wood into a regal-looking fishing boat.

I liked this contact with the members of Amma's family. In their own way, they were connected to Amma's steadily growing mission. I could feel the love and reverence they now had for this extraordinary daughter, sister, whom they had been unable to recognize or to understand during the early years.

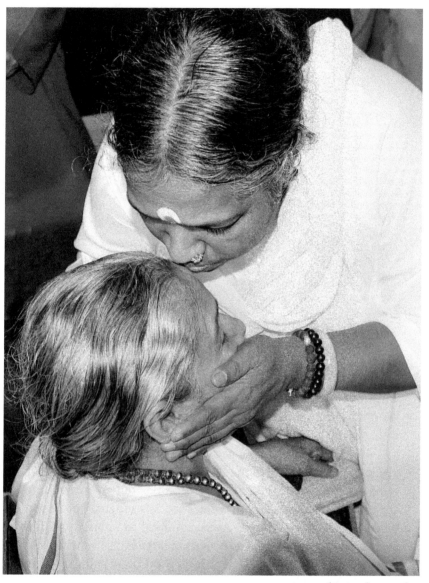

Amma kissing her mother

18

A ROOM WITH A VIEW

I am playing the play of life
The play of the Truth and the Mask
From joy of life and fear of death
The play of a life in the mirror of the ONE.

Prabha

After a few years of romantic living in that damp hut made of woven palm fronds, I began to notice rheumatic pains in my body. My roommate, Theresa, and I decided to find a room in the east wing of the temple, which at the time was still under construction. We discovered a small annex in the second floor and asked Amma if that could be our new home.

Amma said no, but suggested that she would turn the storage space located next to the Kali shrine into a room for us. We were overjoyed, and right after the Europe Tour we moved into the unique, small space whose entrance was situated on the rear balcony of the Kali Temple. Amma allowed us to build in a few extras, and so we became the owners of large built-in shelves and enjoyed the luxury of two windows. A coconut palm stood in front of one window and gifted us daily with the sight of its lush greenery. The windows also allowed us a full view of the large space that had been filled with sand during our nightly seva and on which the new darshan hall was to stand.

I was now living bang in the middle of the daily and nightly goings-on at Amritapuri, because, from the other window, I had a clear view of Amma's courtyard and the spiral steps through which she came to the Kali temple. I heard every sound and was always ready, even at night, to be at Amma's side.

One night during the *Onam* festival I heard soft, happy giggling outside in front of the window where the palm tree stood. My glance fell upon a large swing hung between two palm trees. A circle of delighted brahmacharinis surrounded the swing, which consisted of two ropes and a seat made out of a long wooden slab. Amma was sitting in the middle of this swing with two girls placed one on each side. Seated like this, Amma carried both of them high into the sky.

What a wonderful party that was! Celebrated privately and only for the girls, right there in the middle of the sleeping ashram! The center point of course was Amma, who laughingly invited them for a ride on the swing, to touch the fronds of the palm trees,

Onam swing

and the star-studded sky. Strong arms pushed or slowed down the large, simply-built swing. The girls and women stood by longingly, hoping to take the next ride on the swing with Amma. They whispered to each other softly about the goings on, eyes glowing. I might not have been a young brahmacharini, but nothing could keep me in my room. Armed with my camera, (later I will tell the story of becoming Amma's photographer) I flew rather than walked down the spiral steps and into this precious, joyous celebration. I was noticed right away, and laughingly transformed myself immediately into "the photographer" trying hard to capture the image of the swing moving swiftly back and forth with its three precious occupants.

The darkness was often punctuated by the light from my flash, but what images it captured, or whether anything at all was on the celluloid film in my small Olympus camera was a complete mystery in those 'pre-digital' days. It is only due to Amma's Grace that the impossible became possible and a picture exists as witness to that unique time spent together with Amma on the Onam swing. Even I got a chance to sit next to Amma on that large plank of wood and I allowed her to carry me high into the skies with her.

In the course of time I developed a sixth sense for Amma's nightly celebrations. Even just a gentle, soft whisper that ran through the Ashram, or the sound of several footsteps gliding quickly through the sand or the hall was enough for me to be wide awake, and out in search of the secret gathering. Thus, I found Amma one night happily sitting in the sand, with a few helpers , working cow dung and hay into round flat patties. Her skillful hands moved fast.

She showed no aversion for the specially perfumed material she was handling. Every now and then she giggled and called out loudly like a child at play: "Chapati, chapati, come, we are making chapatis," and then turned back to devote her complete attention to this creative endeavor.

Well, these chapatis did not go to the kitchen! They were carefully dried and later stacked up in front of the Kali Temple,

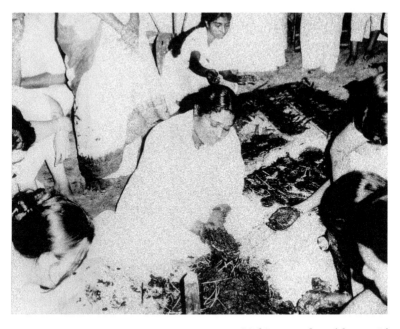

Making cow dung 'chappatis'

lit and slowly burned to a pile of ashes. This ash, placed into small envelopes, Amma would distribute to all the devotees as holy ash during *Shivaratri*, the festival honoring Lord Shiva. In the truest sense of the word, Amma had given us a demonstration of transformation – from cow dung to holy ash. It left a deep impression on our minds!

Up to the year 2,000, many such nightly work projects were undertaken at the ashram. It was much easier to carry sand and help out with the temple construction at night without the scorching sun. Work that was not completed during the day, such as folding the ashram publication, *Matruvani*, would be brought to a finish in the cool hours after midnight. Then the magazines would be sent out all over India, and later even to America and Europe. Time usually ran out before the day the magazine was to be posted and every hand was used to fold the printed pages into a booklet. Amma often sat with the brahmacharinis at the long tables, folding, laughing and always ready for some spiritual

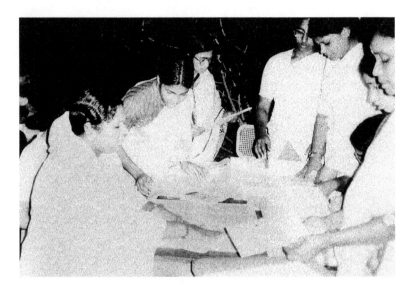

Folding Matruvani papers

jokes and innocent fun. Her youthful looks, voice and gestures made her blend in with them, and magically a light-hearted mood prevailed at the tables. This, combined with a sense of togetherness and belonging, made the huge mountain of paper that still needed folding seem less daunting.

What I really liked about our early years in the ashram was that Amma made use of our skills in various ways. She taught us that no work was demeaning if we had the correct perspective; nothing was too high or too low for us. What was important was to be fully present and involved in the action, because only this would lead to inner growth. Disregarding success or failure, we had many opportunities to experience our strengths and weaknesses and to see our limitations.

Amma repeatedly reminded us to be fully present while doing our seva, and to expect neither reward nor praise. Reciting the mantra that Amma had given helped us tame the mind to some extent. Through the mantra, we tried to keep the mind in the present and prevent it from wandering off. I experienced several times

Collecting gravel

that by surrendering to the moment my thoughts would lose their control over me. My actions became directed by an inexplicable power that arose in me and made me open to new experiences.

So, along with my work as a cook, I also learned precision and stamina while folding printed paper, correctly selecting and sorting construction material at the temple construction site, and using the machine that ground the ingredients for Ayurvedic preparations. I became proficient in passing fresh cement in containers made of old car tires, artfully balancing loads of magazines in my arms as I walked up and down the temple steps, cleaning the temple early in the morning before the first archana and waking up brahmacharis who had spent the night in there because all the huts were occupied. These were some of the many tasks I learned to do with joy and enthusiasm.

In Amritapuri I also discovered that objects can multitask. A large cooking vessel could be used to carry sand or wash clothes. An old plastic bag could stop a leak in the roof made of woven palm leaves, or become a container to grow plants. Old cement sacks could be sewn together to make a privacy screen. This way of living made a deep impression on me. I now began to let go of my hard and fast concepts. I began each day with a sense of adventure, without any expectation or prejudices. This attitude gave me the ability to make the best of unexpected, unfamiliar situations. It is the result of Amma's ways of teaching. Her lessons are not mere book learning, but a new way of life, which became deeply ingrained in me.

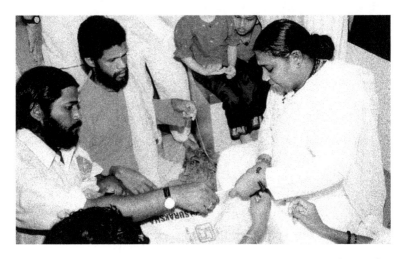

Sewing cement sacks together

19

LIGHT WITHIN AND WITHOUT

She is the Mother,
Christ in me. His very image.
Welcome, Anna Christ she says
And takes my heart into her being.

Prabha

Ritual fire at the Kalari

*Within you, tremendous wisdom is waiting for your per-
mission to unfold. But it will happen only if you allow it.
The real meaning of life is to realize the Divine residing
within you. There are many things which, in your current
state of awareness, you do not know. But as your search
intensifies, you are confronted with new experiences and
situations. New patterns of life will unfold and bring you
closer to your own Self.*

Amma

Amma was born under the star *Karthika*. This special day of
her birth star is celebrated with ritual splendor at the Kalari in
Amritapuri every month. The famous small Krishna temple from
the early years of the ashram is decorated with flower garlands,
origami figures made from palm leaves, oil lamps and other

ornamentation. For one such celebration, I sat with many others on the mats laid out on the temple veranda, closed my eyes and surrendered to the puja songs. In the center of a large colorful *mandala* stood a tall oil lamp decorated with flower garlands. Several smaller lamps burned brightly around this lamp. I watched with fascination as the priest offered flowers with precision to the tall lamp lit with several wicks as each mantra was recited. Its glow lit the faces of the many people who were present, dipping the meditating crowd in a warm light and reminding them to connect with the light in their heart and enter the inner temple.

The burning lights of Karthika beckoned me with their golden hues to turn inwards towards the light in my own heart. All of a sudden I realized that Amma and light are one and the same. That she is not only light but also the source of all light. She has taken birth on the day of Karthika to lead humankind to discover the light in our own hearts and become what we really are.

A picture from the past came to my mind. I was with Amma in Sweden, the last destination on the Europe Tour before we returned to Amritapuri. Twenty happy ashramites and I spent the time before our flight to India with Amma in a picturesque country home on the banks of a fjord. I was busy in the kitchen and could see through the window out onto a magical wild garden that glowed in the light of the morning sun.

It was as if the flowers, the birds, the bushes and the grass had joined together to welcome the new day in the light of the rising sun. And in the middle of this glorious sight sat Amma on a swing that hung from long ropes in an old oak tree.

Silently, her eyes closed, Amma swung in the light of the breaking dawn, immersed in her world of unending bliss and peace. The wind played with the folds of her white dress, gently touching her hair. The canopy of leaves above her head danced. The golden rays of the sun reflected on her luminous face and warmed her tiny feet, which peeked out now and then from under her fluttering white dress. Thus, gracefully, Amma let the swing carry her between heaven and earth.

I slowly walked close to her, wanting to capture this moment in my heart and never lose that divine picture.

As I later sat on the banks of the fjord, the picture of the silent Amma on the swing still echoed in my mind's eye. I could see it in the water, in each wave. The gulls, the trees, the clouds in the sky, all seemed to reflect the glow I had seen earlier on Amma's blissful face. In that moment I knew that the essence behind Amma's form is pure consciousness. The light of this consciousness is the very foundation of creation. In the small physical body of Amma dressed in white lives a world Mother who is one with consciousness from which universes take birth and die. She is one with the eternal pristine Self, the glowing divine light!

And how small I was in this vision! My personal world sank into this all-encompassing Love. Everything in this world that seemed important lost meaning. I became an atom in the universe, a speck of dust in this game of creation and destruction, tiny yet all-pervading. I knew I was connected to the greatest mystery of the world – one that pervades every atom of creation and shines in every human heart.

Amma once told me, "Amma does not see this face," pointing to my face with its changing masks and moods. Pointing to my heart she continued, "Amma sees this face."

"What could Amma read in the face of my heart?" I asked myself. She sees everything there. She sees my beauty and my shadows, my joys and my sorrows and my lies. She sees the walls I have erected and the watchtowers I have built. But behind all this, deep in my very core, she sees her own face. This is how Amma receives every being that comes to her. She says:

> *The Outer Mother exists only to help you to reach the Inner Mother who is absolute consciousness. Silence is the language of this mother who is without attributes. You cannot even call her 'Mother'. 'Mother' is a name and in consciousness there is neither name nor form.*

Amma knows that every soul is longing for its true home, longing to return to the light of consciousness, and so she plays the role of our mother and serves as an example of an awakened being in whose presence we can progress on the path to our true nature.

What does Amma see when she looks at you?

However, it is up to us to overcome our thoughts, which tumble and thunder like a wild mountain stream through our being, continuously creating the game that we call life. In this drama of projections, we are able to see only the outer mother.

This mother will not give up her work till we have learned to silence our thoughts and sink deeper into the stillness of the heart, where the Inner Mother has always been waiting for us. In this stillness we will be able to understand the message of the following story which Amma tells:

In the capitol of one country, in the large market square, stood a huge statue of a Saint with outstretched arms. At the base of the statue was a sign that read:

COME INTO MY ARMS

Soon this land was at war and bombs destroyed the city. The statue was heavily injured in one such attack. Both arms were destroyed. After the war the citizens dedicated themselves to rebuilding the city. This included dealing with the statue. Some residents considered tearing it down completely.

One person said, "No, it is enough if we give the old statue new arms."

But an old wise man said, "We should leave the statue as it is."

Everyone turned to him in astonishment and protested, "Don't you see that the Saint does not have any arms left, but the sign on the statue says, "Come into my arms"?

"I see it," answered the man, "Leave everything as it is. We only need to add these words to the sign:

I HAVE NO OTHER ARMS AND HANDS THAN YOURS."

Amma always reminds us that we are, in reality, divine beings in human bodies. Love, compassion and incredible power lie dormant within us, waiting to find expression.

Even before I met Amma, I came to know this truth at a spiritual retreat. We were a group of seekers gathered in the large meditation room of a farmhouse. One morning we were asked a question and were supposed to conscientiously write down our

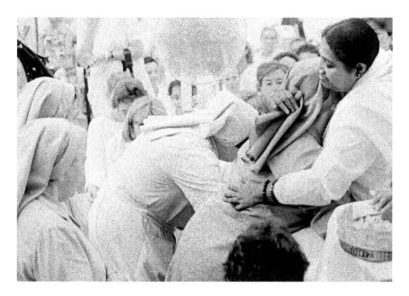

Darshan in Spain

answers. I tightly held my pencil and paper in my hand and heard the teacher ask: "Who am I?"

We all looked at each other in surprise. Well, who am I? Certainly this "I" did not refer to my name, occupation or status in society. That was easy to figure out. But then, who was I without these attributes? At that moment I was an open vessel waiting for the answer to be placed into it.

My eyes searched out the eyes of a saint whose picture hung on the wall next to me. I did not know then that this saint was Ramana Maharshi, and that his teaching involved the technique of self-inquiry, of continuously asking ourselves this question: "Who am I?" Amma had not yet entered my life, but today I can say for sure that Amma's eyes shine with light just like those of Ramana. His eyes spoke to me and said: "You are God." I, God? I was instantly uncomfortable with this thought and my conscience struggled with this definition. Is that not blasphemy? I thought of the fairy tale of the fisherman and his wife who always wanted more. I saw myself as the fisherwoman who was punished because she wanted to be God. I saw images of all those wise women who

Dancing in Sveden

were burned or crucified and I wished I could erase the words that Ramana Maharshi spoke. Therefore, I wrote "God's image" on my paper.

There is one word too many on your slip of paper, said the teacher as he read my answer.

I need a lot of strength and courage on my journey, but I have trust in Amma, who always encourages us to accept what is, regardless of whether it is pleasant or hurtful, beautiful or ugly, friend or foe. With endless patience she shows us the way to a life in which everyone who has made his ego a zero is a hero.

She is teaching me how to live in the moment. She teaches me how to accept my joys, sorrows, love, shortcomings, stupidity and much more, safe in the knowledge that all these are not reality but the stuff of my ego. It defines my figure playing on the large board game known as life. I experience happiness when this figure moves with ease on earth. I feel anxious when it loses its way, and cry with it when the pain is too much to bear. Every day I share joy, sorrow, elation and disappointment with this figure. It is an illusion that I have fully identified with, become one with.

Even then, I know that deep within me burns the light of eternal consciousness, which is my true nature. I am on the journey to this light. May my life be a path to it.

I play the game of imagining and judging,
Of thinking and wishing of the past and the future.
I play the game of bottomless sorrow and dancing joy,
This game is my journey to the game without players
Where you and I are ONE in the open space of my heart.

Prabha

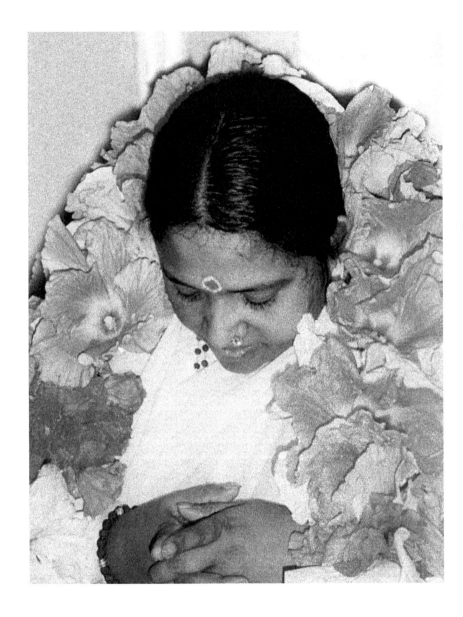

20

THE PHOTOGRAPHER

Touch the earth, bloom in dance,
Sow the seeds from the depths of your being.
Trembling, you shall see the blossoms reach the skies.

Prabha

My life as Amma's photographer began with an enchanting picture that I effortlessly captured with the camera of my heart for eternity. A laughing Amma, standing in a small garden between tall rose bushes in full bloom, joining both hands above her head in a gesture of bowing down.

This magical garden belonged to Amma's ashram in Reunion and lay right in front of the tiny house where Amma stayed during her programs on that small island in the Indian Ocean. Amma was on her way to her room after a long morning of giving darshan. The open rose petals glistened in glorious colors and caressed Amma's small form clothed in white. Her eyes reflected light from the darshan she had given to hundreds of people of different ethnicities. The huge crowds that had come to see her were gathered in the big ashram hall with its beautiful pictures and carvings, to get their hugs. This island had been occupied by the French for a long time and sheltered along with Europeans, also Creoles, people whose ancestors had set foot on this island as slaves.

Amma laughed as she waved goodbye and her beaming face spoke to us silently: "I will soon be back to be with you all." I was deeply touched by the unsurpassed beauty of this moment. I knew without a doubt that Amma was an enlightened being, eternal, powerful, yet soft as a rose. I longed for nothing else but to own a picture of her in that setting.

Of course, I was aware that I did not have permission to photograph Amma, but I immediately saw my small Olympus camera in my mind's eye. It lay neatly packed among my other meager belongings in a suitcase, which I had left behind in Switzerland.

The next year when we came to Reunion, the camera was there with me.

On the very first day I asked Amma during darshan: "Amma, may I take a picture of you as you walk through the rose garden?" "You may take pictures of me," she said, and smiled mysteriously as I quickly left to get the camera from my room.

I wanted to be ready for the rose-garden picture, and so I excitedly stood holding the camera in my hands long before darshan was over, following Amma's every move. Finally, Amma got up and, surrounded by several visitors, stood on the veranda of the ashram. She was having a serious discussion with someone, and I tried to make myself as inconspicuous as possible. I looked for the best angle on the path that led through the rose garden and waited there.

Unfortunately, I was on a hunt for a moment from the past and was deeply disappointed. This year is not last year and Amma's picture in the rose garden looked different. She still continued to talk to the people on the veranda as she walked by, but her face wore a serious look.

My finger did not click a single time on the shutter button. Of course I was disappointed, but a joke someone had recently told me came to mind: "Do you want to know how to make God laugh? Tell him your plans!"

Yes, indeed, my plans had failed, but there was still an unused 36-frame roll of Kodak film in my camera! Did Amma not say that I could take her pictures? "Pictures" means more than one picture! Why should I be so upset if today was not the same as last year?

The next day when Amma entered the darshan room and the swamis recited the mantras during the *pada puja*, I watched the scene through the camera lens with fascination and a little nervousness. This time my finger clicked on the shutter button several times. Amma ignored what I was doing, and for me this meant she approved.

After two days I had filled half the Kodak roll with pictures of Amma, and my curiosity to see the results had reached its peak. I could hardly wait to see on glossy paper whether I had been successful, so I set out to a town nearby in search of a photo studio. Today in the digital age I can instantly check my pictures so my patience is not pushed to its limits. I do not have to spend hours in nail-biting suspense waiting for the results of my labor, or make last-minute dicey trips to photo studios to have the film developed as soon as possible. Bargaining for a good price, the intense feeling while waiting for the treasure, the heart palpitations while opening up the packet of photos – all these now belong to the past. With digitization I lost a valuable instrument for checking my patience, revealing my illusions and my fears, and intensely experiencing unexpected, spontaneous joy.

Dancing in Réunion

In Saint Louis de la Réunion I found a likeable Frenchman in a small shop, who, with a beaming smile, handed the photos to me after two days. Astonished, I looked down at gorgeous pictures of Amma. It was almost as if the camera had a mind of its own and had positioned itself at the most advantageous angles and clicked at exactly the right moment to obtain such perfect results. The first photo I held in my hand is on the cover of this book.

In the evening when Amma was on her way to a temple in the mountains, I brought my treasure to her car window. After she had taken a look at the pictures she said to Swamini: "Prabha sees my various moods. I would like her to take my pictures from now on." Turning to me she continued: "You should not stop taking Amma's pictures, not even if she scolds you."

Ever since that day there is a Western photographer named Prabha around Amma, the most beautiful and exciting subject in the world. And there is the student Prabha around Amma the Master, the hottest fire ever designed to burn our ego. Amma gave me, with a seva as her photographer, a chance to be exactly there where I had always wanted to be – at a place of transformation. Along with the countless images transformed by light on celluloid into glowing pictures of Amma, my mind was and continues to be slowly transformed through living and working for Amma, who resides in my heart as that brilliant form in the rose garden.

Understand that the creation and the Creator are not two.
Just as gold exists in and through all gold jewelry,
so too the Creator pervades the entirety of this creation.
If we can cultivate such an understanding, we will never lose
sight of our inherent unity.

Amma

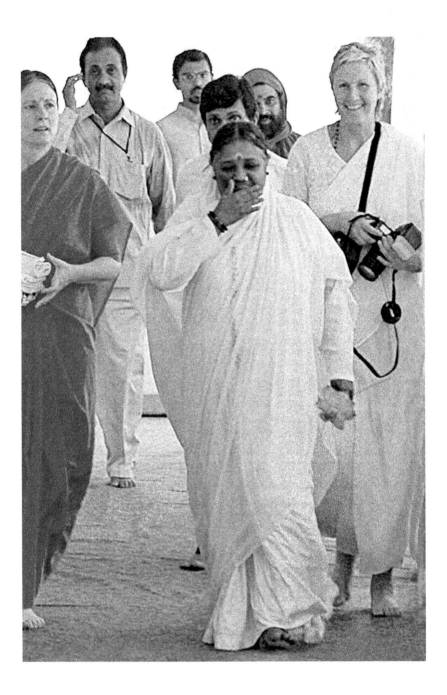

21

TWO COLLEAGUES IN THE
PHOTO BUSINESS

My garden was perfect, designed my own way.
Now it is dry, a desert, empty.
A gaping hole ... If only it were space?
A space, to invite you into?

Prabha

After Amma gave me some time to get accustomed to the ins and outs of the seva as her photographer, she set the next stage of the game in motion. She sent me a colleague: Janani, mother of the universe, a strong, successful woman by whom I immediately felt threatened. Instead of becoming colleagues, we became opponents.

Actually we understood each other pretty well and were on the same wavelength in many ways. We were able to hold meaningful conversations with one another even about our petty jealousies and fights, but were unable to resolve these differences. Today, in retrospect, I can see what a perfect gift it was from Amma, this very latest ego-basher, the 'Janani-Prabha Game'!

Janani often gave me reason to be jealous and, on occasion, to cry tears of disappointment which I tried my best to conceal.

Amma and the swamis found my childish crying and tantrums hilarious and often consciously escalated our dramas and competition. Amma was masterful at plucking on the tense strings of the instrument, named 'my ego,' and was able to draw out some awful, discordant notes from it. Amma worked on all aspects of my personality with sensitivity, created difficult test situations, never passed up a chance to teach, was eternally focused on

growth and transformation, never on destroying anything other than the ego. It is both incomprehensible and unbelievable to see how she does this.

Each photo we released had first to be approved by Amma. This meant in addition to the long hours of darshan, reading hundreds of letters, advising the people who ran the various institutions and humanitarian works, Amma also had to spend time on Janani's and my small, but for us important, joys and sorrows. On both sides joy meant: "Amma accepted my picture and declined yours." What sorrow meant – that's easy to figure out, right?

One day, Amma sent me a message that I should purchase a reflex camera. With this new technical accessory I accompanied Amma on the Australia Tour, carrying the new camera in a big grey bag slung over my shoulder. The venue for the first program was by the sea. By nightfall I lay happily tucked away in my cozy bed in the small vacation home, well fed and looked after by a nice Amma devotee. Listening at night to the waves that were so close made me feel intimately connected to nature. Knowing that Amma, whom I would see the next morning, was also close by filled me with joy and contentment.

The next morning, I happily shouldered my new Nikon and was driven to the program hall by my host. Soon I would be taking some amazing pictures with my new camera. Life could not get any better!

Sadly, I had spoken too soon. My happiness evaporated into thin air when I discovered that Janani had slept in the same house as Amma.

She proudly accompanied Amma to the program, filmed Amma (for she also did video) and took a few pictures. I plummeted from my recent high and distractedly tried to click a few shots. As Amma entered the building, walking close to me, I tried my best to conceal my deep disappointment. Soon stillness and peace spread throughout the darshan hall. People meditated, the swamis sang, and Amma hugged. I sat all the way at the back in a corner. While I pretended to meditate, my thoughts flew about, uncontrolled in all directions, getting darker and more negative by the minute.

In my mind's eye, a scenario played out: I saw Amma and Janani going together for a walk in the picturesque surroundings. Janani was taking pictures and laughing. Amma also laughed and even called Janani to her room where she was allowed to take beautiful close-ups of Amma. In one of these portraits Amma gazed directly into the camera. Janani now clicked the most popular, most desirable Amma portrait that all devotees longed for, the "*direct look*"!

The very same Prabha who woke up so happy in that small house on the beach was now a confused, uncontrolled bundle of childish jealousy. While Amma was pouring her whole being into lovingly hugging one person after another, huge battles were

being waged in my mind. Externally calm, but internally furious, wound up and driven by a strong impulse, I asked someone for directions to Amma's house. After I discovered that it was hardly a kilometer away, I picked up my bag with the Nikon and made my way there. Black clouds of fury had gathered within me. I felt myself discriminated against and tricked by Amma. Jealousy gnawed at me and I heard my ego say: "Not so fast, Amma. Not with me. I don't care who takes the pictures, but it most certainly won't be me anymore. You tricked me."

It was in this mood that I entered the house where Amma was staying. The doors were open. I could hear someone bustling around in another part of the house as I softly walked through the hallway and spied Amma's room. No one else was in sight. The coast was clear when I lightly tiptoed inside with the Nikon and left it on Amma's bedside table. Upon it I placed a hastily written note: "For Amma, from Prabha."

Well, mission accomplished, as they say. I left the house unnoticed. My mind was a few steps ahead of me, already picturing the scene when Amma would walk into the room, see the camera, discover my note and read it, and what she would then proceed to say and do.

Driven by such thoughts I hardly realized where I was headed, and was surprised to find myself standing in front of the darshan hall. I entered and noticed the long lines of people on both sides of Amma, the tones of the melodious bhajans that filled the room, and Amma's energy which also encompassed me, the rebel.

I told myself that I was satisfied and had only done the needful. With cake and coffee from the Bistro run by the devotees, I stuffed down the nagging doubt I had in me and pretended to be at peace with myself and the world at large. In the meantime, I was also covertly watching Janani who seemed to have no clue about my little adventure.

In the evening, Amma and the swamis again arrived at the hall with Janani in tow. But my Nikon was nowhere to be seen. My doubts had in the interim intensified into self-pity. I huddled the entire evening near Amma and my mind played out in many versions the drama of wounded Prabha, a four-hour long play of sorrow and rage. Incidentally, I was completely unaware that similar dramas had played out through my entire life. That night Amma did not speak a single word to me. Now and then I felt her glance upon me. Finally, towards the end of darshan the curtain fell upon my drama, and my inner theatrics came to an end.

Amma hugged me silently before she climbed into the car that was to drive her to a house visit. Janani was also there with Amma, but who cares, my drama was over. I walked fast through the night to Amma's house, found the doors wide open, stepped into Amma's room and saw that the Nikon was still there where I had placed it yesterday. Only the note had been moved. It now lay on another small table.

I left the house softly, surreptitiously, just as I had entered. The bag with the Nikon, the starry sky, and my hurrying steps through the sleeping landscape, all felt so good and belonged to me, just as the inner struggle of the past few days also belonged to me. I felt this struggle had most certainly changed something inside me for the better. My hostess was cleaning up at the program hall, and together we drove to the small home on the cliff, against whose rocks the ocean roared, accompanying me into a dreamless sleep.

Devoid of life and love
The energy flies past the heart.
Buzzing endlessly, cold, calculating
Full of anxious past, in my head.

Prabha

22

THE GAME IS OVER

When the sun of the Self
Illuminates the struggle in me,
Then, there you are,
In the heart of my heart.

Prabha

The 'Janani-Prabha Game' took several years to run its course, and we two adult women were absolutely helpless in its grip. We simply could not find the switch to turn off this merry-go-round. I often asked myself what the saying "Your worst enemy is your best friend" meant for me. Surely, it did not apply to me, but rather to a completely surrendered person who could show his enemy the other cheek after he had been slapped on the first. I most definitely did not belong to this category of people. Today, however, after our game has come to an end, I know that Janani was my best friend in my journey as a seeker. My personality was pitted against hers, and through our struggles many old patterns were broken up and swept away. The burden of my ego became lighter and I gained more clarity over my inner landscape.

The day finally dawned when Amma put an end to the conflict that had plagued our relationship. It was high time for this to happen because I could no longer imagine spending months, years, or most urgently the upcoming Europe Tour with an opponent rather than a colleague. At the time I was again living in Switzerland, but spent a lot of time in the ashram. I photographed a lot and still stayed in the small room right next to the Kali shrine, next to the Goddess who had to work so hard to destroy my ego.

I, too, had to work hard on that particular day. It was high season for Indian weddings, since the stars were well placed for these arranged alliances, and I captured images of several couples and their families with my camera during the traditional rituals. Several newly married couples were now waiting longingly for the pictures, which I had to process as quickly as possible. Up to my neck in work, I asked Janani if she would be the photographer for the next event. A lot of parents had registered for the traditional

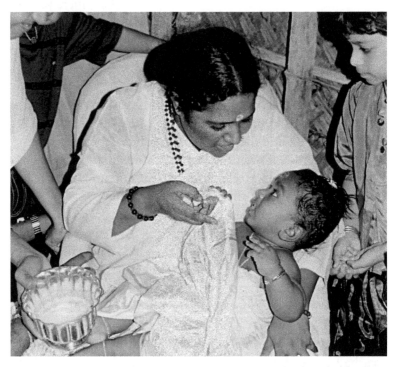

First solid food for this baby

first feeding, where Amma would feed the babies a mouthful of their first solid food. Many of them, clad in fine *mundus*, were waiting more or less patiently for a mouthful of the sweet rice pudding. Janani would be taking pictures of this auspicious ceremony.

She gladly agreed because this gave her a chance to be close to Amma and have her fill of the pulsating life around her. I busied myself with processing the pictures, and from my window saw Janani cross Amma's courtyard to get to the darshan hall. Soon the phone in my room rang and one of the swamis asked me to come to the stage because it was time for the baby feeding.

"I am not coming today. Janani is there," I said and turned back to the computer. The swami, however, would not agree; he wanted Prabha there and not Janani, who, by the way, happened to be standing next to him waiting to take the pictures. I argued, but only in vain. This initiated the breakdown of the Janani-Prabha game. I knew this drama was no longer necessary. I had suffered

enough, had been egoistic, achieved insight and clarity. Now I had outgrown the game just as a little girl outgrows her toy puppet.

I came on stage with my camera, saw Amma surrounded by happy people who would soon sink into her arms, saw the pleased look on the swamis' faces and the disappointment on Janani's. She

Waiting for Amma in Tamil Nadu

was hurt and quickly tried to walk past me and leave the stage. But I stopped her, whispered to her to accompany me and brought her directly in front of Amma, who looked surprised to see the two of us standing right in front of her, dancing out of step. "Amma," I said without skipping a beat, "Janani and I want to be friends."

Amma's eyes widened and a mischievous smile spread over her face. Turning to the people near her, she said: "Look at these two. They are always fighting. If Amma looks at one, then the other one is unhappy. If she looks at the other, then the first one is sad." Laughing, she jabbed both her forefingers against each other and said loudly: "Janani, Prabha … fighting, fighting!"

Still holding on tightly to Janani, I said earnestly, "Amma, that was before. Then we were still babies, but now we are all grown up!"

As Amma laughed again, I heard myself pleading, "Amma, please make a *sankalpa* so that Janani and I can be friends." It suddenly became very quiet around Amma. The Indians standing near her whispered: "Sankalpa. Prabha would like your sankalpa, Amma." Many others nodded their heads. Amma gazed for a long time, upon these two women who had come together under such difficult circumstances.

"Okay," she said lovingly. And that was it! Amma's sankalpa, her caring support, worked. After the dissolution of the Janani-Prabha Game, her sankalpa made us into two colleagues who treat each other with care and respect. Janani and I are even today bound to each other by a loving friendship. I thank Amma from the bottom of my heart that she played this game with us so skillfully. In my heart I have a special place for Janani. I have a lot to thank her for, and I send her a warm hug.

23

SWIMMING IN THE RIVER

Imagine the Divine, a pure and full river
whose waters clean dirty canals and stagnant pools,
Purifying everything that touches it.

Amma

During my first trip with Amma I sat all the way at the back in the small ashram bus, which seated about 30 people. The two seats to the left of the front entrance were reserved for Amma and Swamini Amma. No one sat on Amma's seat whenever she occasionally left the bus to travel with a devotee in their car. Her asana always lay on her seat and gave us the feeling that she was physically with us.

The bus often stopped on the side of the road. We would watch full of hope, while Amma stepped out of a comfortable car and climbed into the bus to laugh, meditate, recite mantras, tell stories, or travel in silence through Mother India with us.

That day we were driving to a program in the state of Tamil Nadu. Amma was the last person to climb in. Her gaze immediately fell on the last seat, situated directly above the exhaust pipe and without a window to close. Her glittering eyes connected with mine for a fraction of a second and I could feel her sympathy for the newcomer in the group (me!) who had got the worst seat in the bus.

I was not worried by the fact that my sari slowly turned grey. The joy that filled my heart helped me see only beauty everywhere. I looked with wonder and fearlessness out of the window, despite Swami Ramakrishnanandas's breakneck driving style, as he boldly steered our bus through the crowded streets. Our destination was Coimbatore, a city about a six-hour drive from the ashram. As we drove, the landscape became green and the houses, sparse. Our bus stopped in front of a large bridge, and I saw several fellow travelers running towards a river. The words "Oh, we are going swimming!" rippled through our bus, and soon the seats were empty as all of us were pulled along in the swift current of devoted women running after Amma in the garden of a big house on the bank of the river.

After quickly removing our saris, we tied up the underskirts above our chests and followed Amma who was already standing in her red swim-dress on the steps. Before we dove into the peacefully flowing river, we cupped a little water in our palms and let it slowly flow over our heads. This holy ritual connected us symbolically with the water that would soon accept us into it. My first swim with Amma was simply magical. I can clearly picture her with her long hair loose, the graceful movements of her body as she swam, and her infectious laughter. It seemed to me as if all the river goddesses on this planet were embodied in Amma's form.

After we had swum happily for a while, laughing and playing like innocent children, Amma called for her soap, a perfumed French concoction someone had given her, and we women washed her long wavy hair with it. The soap lathered in our hands, Amma laughed and played the recalcitrant child by suddenly diving into the water and washing the soap out of her hair before we were finished. After that, it was our turn. No, Amma did not wash our hair. She caught hold of each one of us, and used her soap to wash our faces with purposeful strokes, and dunk us in the water with lightning speed. She then called out loudly: "*Vasana* cleaning, vasana cleaning!" This meant Amma was cleaning us of some of the many things, that are an obstacle to realizing the divinity in us.

I would have stayed in the water forever, but Amma asked us to hurry up, and we quickly got into our clothes and onto the bus to continue driving to our destination, where the program was to take place the very same evening in a large hall.

It was almost 2am that night when we drove back to Amritapuri. This time I was standing right in the front of the bus near Amma, peering into the darkness. I was happy and content, enjoying the physical closeness to Amma.

Ramakrishnananda Swami continued to display his Formula 1 driving style as we raced through quiet streets. Suddenly I heard Amma call out, making him brake before a long curve of the road, just in time to bring us to a halt in front of a huge herd of buffaloes. The animals ignored us completely and took their own cool time to amble across the road and make way for our vehicle to continue on its journey back home to the ashram in Vallikavu.

Vasana cleaning

A boatman ferried us across the water in the dim light of dawn. In the ashram I lay down on my mat and disappeared into a deep, dreamless sleep, waking up only when the sun stood high in the sky. In those few moments when I lay awake before getting up, my mind replayed the memory of our swim in the river, and along with it I heard Amma's words:

> *"The master is like a river. You can stand on the banks of the river, praising it and its beauty. However, whatever you may say about the glory of the river has no real meaning as long as you yourself do not dive into it. To surrender to a Master and jump into this river requires courage. The currents will carry you unceasingly and directly to the ocean - to God, or your real Self."*

We have swum in many rivers in India with Amma, in small and large ones, in sacred and insignificant ones. What always stands out are our prayers and games in the waters, and Amma's words. She masterfully taught us that life and love are not two separate entities but a single united one. That the path to the light in our hearts lies in flowing along with life, aligned with its higher values and by discovering joy in service to others.

We often recited the *Gayatri* mantra, standing with Amma in the water. Forming a bowl with our palms held together, we scooped water into it and held it close to our heart. After the closing words of the mantra we then poured this purified water over our heads. Finally we all dived deep into the water. We repeated this ritual over and over again every time we stopped with Amma for a swim. It cleansed us, opened our hearts and helped us experience a deep connection to everything around us.

There are many forms of therapy that claim to free us of inner impressions, defense mechanisms, and dependencies formed mostly in our childhood. Amma knows the reality about each one of us, and has her own methods of showing us new paths and teaching us to walk on these paths. In her energy, things fall in line and an opening takes place. The new is born; the old disappears. We realize the preciousness of our life and our love for creation.

If you make God a part of your life, it will be sanctified and have a healing influence on the life of others. Imagine the Divine as a fully flowing, pure river, cleaning the dirty pools and stagnant waters within you.

Amma

24

THE BHAVANI AND THE SMALL RIVER

My favorite place to swim was at the confluence of the rivers
Bhavani and Kauveri in Tamil Nadu. The ruins of an old temple
stand at this site and wide stone steps lead into the sacred water.
I remember the first time we took a dip at this holy bathing *ghat*.
In spite of the somber presence of the temple nearby, we played
with childlike abandon in the warm waters. We loudly sang the
Lalitha Sahasranama Stotram, dove, laughed and felt a complete

connection with Bhavani, the holy mother, and Amma, our spiritual mother. A palpable lightheartedness suffused our every move. Filled with innocent joy, we turned into spontaneous children.

We had the space by the river all to ourselves. No one washed clothes or large trucks in the water. Goddess Bhavani had granted us the gift of time and Amma's timeless beauty – time for games and chanting mantras in the water, time to meditate, to cook and eat. Time to sit on the steps in the evening, warmed by the sun. Time to listen to Amma sing and to hear her words in the dark.

While we swam with Amma in the river, the men who had kitchen duty lit a cooking fire. They and the *ammamars*, the older women who, incidentally, were probably much younger than I, cooked 'Bhavanikanji,' a soup consisting of rice, beans and shredded coconut. We had named this dish after the river Bhavani, and no other soup in the world is as tasty. Its aroma was enhanced by

Bhavani River, meditation after swim

the holiness of the place, the majesty of the river, Amma's presence bubbling over with bliss and our happiness to be so close to her.

I will never forget a picture from this day: Amma in her red swim dress, walking about like a carefree young girl among the various stands on the river steps, shops which sold tea and holy souvenirs. Her curly damp hair hung open and a thin towel covered her shoulders. Someone had handed her an interesting looking instrument of sorts. It was a pipe made of multicolored paper with a mouthpiece at one end. When Amma blew at it, it unfurled like a tiny snake waking up from sleep, and made a high-pitched noise, which I recognized from my trips to the local fair as a child. What a unique picture this was! Amma, in ankle length swim dress, playing on this pipe, with all of us following behind her.

We merrily walked from one stand to the other, Amma still playing on the pipe. As a final reward, Amma bought us all a cup of chai and shared a packet of sweet cookies with us. Who would ever have thought that this girl who moved about so care-freely was Mata Amritanandamayi Devi, one of the greatest saints ever,

the very embodiment of the pure Self? Even as a young child Amma had dedicated herself to the world without ever being part of it. She lives amongst us, plays, laughs, sings, and prays with us. Coming down to our level, she opens the door into our inner depths, healing our sorrows.

That night when we sat on the stone steps and Amma sang in the darkness of the night, I could sometimes intuit in her song and its intense vibration her oneness with all of creation. The sound of her voice contained the river and the sanctity of the old temple. In it were also the stones on which we sat, the sky with its stars, the entire universe, and also Prabha, who felt so small and yet so expansive in Love and Unity with the Whole.

We stayed overnight twice at the Bhavani. I have almost forgotten the first time when I slept on the floor of the tourist pavilion, but I clearly remember the other stay. I travelled in the last bus in Amma's convoy, which was also the oldest and slowest vehicle. I made this trip sitting on a large Indian kitchen machine. A checkered quilt covered this large container and grinding stone and so it served as my seat, and I held onto a metal post inside the bus for support. The roads in India in those days were really bad. At night I tied myself to this pole with a piece of cloth and this way I was even able to sleep for a little while.

About two hours before we reached the Bhavani, the motor of our bus started burning. A black cloud of smoke entered the vehicle and forced us all to abandon it. I was the first one out since my seat was right by the only door at the back of the bus. By the time I got to the source of the smoke, both drivers had opened the hood and were busy dousing the fire with our water bottles. Despondent, we stood next to the bus. I was sure that at this moment the only thing on our minds was Amma and the lost chance to bathe with her in the river Bhavani. Glancing at the motor I casually said, "Start the motor once more." Everyone looked at me in surprise and thought I was rambling in a state of shock. Anyway, one of the men climbed into the driver's cabin and turned the key. And there, our beloved bus, which had carried us through so many states in India, came to life and started up. We all rushed to our seats and the journey continued. Only later, when it became dark quickly, as it does in India, did we discover parts of the machine that powered the headlamps had burned out. It was nothing extraordinary for a vehicle to be on the road in India without headlights. The situation came to a head, however, when we approached the long, narrow white bridge over the river Bhavani, which would lead us to the holy temple and bathing ghat. Not wanting to take the risk of crossing the bridge in the face of oncoming vehicles without functioning headlights, we had to wait by the side for over an hour before being rescued by one of the other ashram vehicles.

All hope of bathing with Amma had been lost. When we finally arrived at the bungalows, it was midnight and our fellow travelers were fast asleep in two of the fully occupied buildings. We saw Amma standing at the door of her room, her face full of sympathy as she informed us that there was no more place in the rented rooms. She told us to sleep outside on the sand forming a circle with our heads facing inside and our legs out, since we might be sharing the space with a bunch of wild pigs who were out and about at night foraging for food. We were disappointed, yet followed Amma's advice and formed a circle, watching our four-legged friends scurrying about for a while before we fell asleep. We awakened the next morning with the rising sun, and our sad feelings from the night before melted into the water as we took our morning bath in the river with Amma.

The locations of the Brahmasthanam Temples, sanctified sites consecrated and blessed by Amma, decide the route of our yearly North India Tour, which takes us through Bombay up to Delhi and further east to Calcutta.

It was much more difficult to find a suitable river for swimming in North India. We were therefore grateful when our vehicles stopped near a small bridge and we climbed down a steep embankment to Amma and her companions who were already waiting by a small stream. The water that meandered through large rocks was cold and we really could not swim there. Nevertheless, we enjoyed the chance to stretch our limbs and take a cooling dip in the water. I was sitting on a mossy stone up to my shoulders in water when I felt an intense pain in my hand, which shot through my entire body.

At exactly this moment I heard Amma calling: "Come quickly out of the water, we don't want to stay here any longer." I could see her already climbing back up the embankment. We women

Delightful Bhavani

hastily wrapped our saris around us. The men had it a little easier and were already back on the road. I had no time to worry about my hurting hand. It was only after I collapsed on my bus seat that I looked at it and recoiled in horror. My thumb, forefinger and half of my middle fingers were fully swollen, looking like large sausages. Panic arose in me. My eyes searched for Amma, but I heard that she had already driven on.

I watched with fear as the swelling increased from minute to minute, spreading to even my ring finger. I consulted a doctor who was on the same bus, and he said, "Well, all you can do now is pray." I had been doing that anyway ever since I discovered my condition. I continued to pray with all my heart for Amma to wait for me and save me from the pain and panic. We had hardly driven for 15 minutes when everyone shouted out: "Look, there's Amma!" Sure enough, Amma sat by a wide, deep river, waiting for me, as I hurried down to the riverbank. There was just enough space between Amma and the river for me to sit down near her and show her my hand. She touched it silently and placed it on her knee. Everyone was talking loudly and wanted to know what had happened to me. Only Amma stayed completely still.

She reached into her long open hair, plucked out a single dark strand, stretched it between thumb and forefinger of both hands and rubbed it slowly on my hand up and down for a while, and continued the ritual with a second strand of hair. By now everyone else was also still and there was pin-drop silence. They watched in awe as Amma gazed deeply into my eyes and said: "Everything will be over in ten hours, but now you are not allowed to have any evening tea or cookies as the others will at four o'clock."

Before I came to Amma I had been the student of a shaman for many years. In the ashram I missed the special shamanic ceremonies, the drum circle, trance dances, the wisdom of the Native Americans and their connection with nature. This was by far the biggest sacrifice I made, even more than giving up my material possessions. Now Amma showed me that she knew this about me, through the healing ritual with her strand of hair. Why else would she have chosen to cure my hand in that manner when a mere look from her would have sufficed to remove the pain and swelling? I was so grateful for this *leela* that I was more than willing to give something in return from my side. So I happily agreed to give up not only the tea and cookies but also my dinner. I returned to the bus, relieved and fearless, secure in the knowledge that Amma was in charge of my hand and it would be fully healed as she had promised.

We stopped again at dusk to have a dinner of *idlis* with Amma. The brahmacharis were keen to know what had bitten me and surrounded Amma to share their wildest speculations with her.

Indian Tour bus, 1995

They kept teasing me even as they hungrily devoured their idlis, "You are not allowed to eat, Prabha. On no account should you eat anything." Little did they know that I was not at all bothered by this fast. On the contrary, because of this entire incident I felt even more connected to Amma. She let me know that she was aware of my shamanic past, yet another testimony to her omniscience. Amma never talked again about what had bitten me in the water, but after ten hours the swelling subsided and I continued the journey with a fully healed hand.

That night when we reached our place to sleep, we found that two suitcases were missing. Thieves had taken them off the top of the bus during the dinner stop while we were all engrossed in speculating with Amma about the mysterious creature that had bitten my hand in the tiny river.

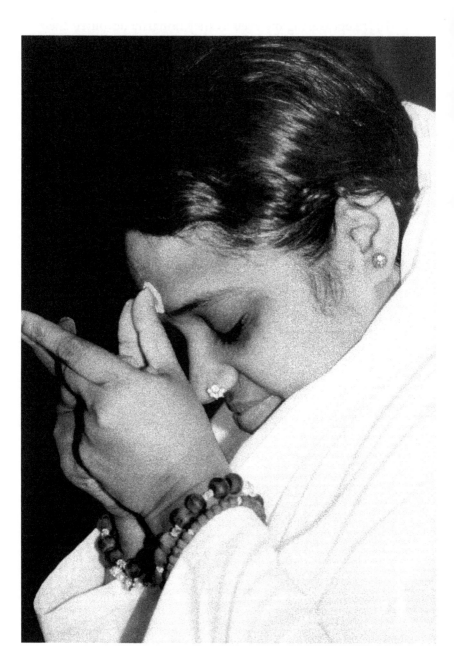

25

GAYATRI-MANTRA

OM

OM BHUR BHUVAH SVAHA
TAT SAVITUR VARENYAM
BHARGO DEVASYA DHIMAHI
DHIYO YO NAH PRACHODAYAT

OM

WE MEDITATE UPON THE BRILLIANCE OF THE DIVINE LIGHT,
THE SUN OF PURE CONSCIOUSNESS, WHICH WE VENERATE.
MAY ITS LIGHT ILLUMINE US
AND MAY WE EXPERIENCE THE HIGHEST TRUTH.

It was many years ago in Australia that I discovered the tremendous spiritual energy invoked by reciting the Gayatri mantra. We were staying with Amma in a house whose garden boasted a unique swimming pool. The edges were lined with large, heavy, reddish-brown lava rock. Broad leaves of various tropical plants that grew along the water shaded the rocks and created the look of a pond set amidst nature. A large wooden float stretched like a peninsula onto the water, which reflected the early morning sky. I decided to spend a few hours that morning there, in meditation.

I was just about to go back into the house when Amma, followed by half a dozen of my Amma sisters, came by for a swim.

Amma sat down next to me on the float and soon was engrossed in a discussion about relationships and children with a young American woman. I paid close attention since I had experienced a relationship and had children. I heard Amma say, "For you, a relationship is okay but better not to have children. In your situation how will you be able to give them sufficient love?"

My awareness shifted the moment I heard Amma's words. The swimming pool vanished and along with it the wooden float we were sitting on. I was transported to my former life as a young woman. Reliving my feelings and emotions from the past, I could picture how I tried so hard to do everything right as a wife and mother, how I tried to love my children and my husband with everything I had. Somehow, through Amma's presence now, all my limitations and barriers to true love were exposed.

I felt so strongly the pain of being trapped in a body ruled by the mind and by my limited ability to love that I burst out crying. I cried for my children, for my family and for all the children and families in this world. I cried over the prison I was in, over the limitations and imprisonment of all human beings. A pain for which

I have yet to find a word swept over me. I felt guilty and yet not guilty, and knew that I shared this fate with the rest of humanity.

I realized that Amma had stretched out and placed her feet in my lap. I held on to her divine feet and bathed them with my tears that poured endlessly from the unending pain in my heart.

As my tears did not stop, Amma asked me firmly to stand up, held me tightly for a short while and then pushed me fully clothed into the water. I dived in deep, still crying, and swam to the other end of the pond. There I hid among the large leaves of the plants growing along the edge. In the meantime, Amma and the others were in the water. They formed a circle, and the sound of them singing the Gayatri mantra reached me. The mantra poured into me like heavenly consolation that gently yet powerfully touched my heart and put an end to my tears. I swam out from my hiding place to Amma and joined the sacred circle of my sisters who were reciting the Gayatri.

26

THE RING

Grant me the grace to bow down,
to bow deep to the earth
so my life may take root
in the field of your Love.

Prabha

I gave birth to my first daughter in South Africa and was full of gratitude, joy and astonishment as I gazed upon the newborn. My husband gifted me a magical ring to celebrate the occasion. It looked like a small flower in whose center was a blue sapphire. Around this, glittered petals made of brilliant diamonds. I imagined that they sparkled with our love for each other and joy over the small family that we had become.

I was sure that I would wear this ring, a priceless testimony to our love, for a lifetime. I could picture myself as a grandmother wearing this piece of jewelry on my wrinkled hand. At that time, I experienced a moment of deep connection and heavenly unity. Unfortunately, the reality was quite different. My husband and I separated when the kids became older, and the ring on my finger was a painful reminder of this unthinkable, unexpected separation. I stopped wearing it, and nine years later, when I met

Amma, I placed the ring, imbued with all my sorrows and joys, in her hand.

At the time, Amma would often wear a ring given to her on Devi Bhava. One day Swamini whispered to me, "The ring you gave Amma is still in her room. Maybe she will wear it tonight." Towards the end of Devi Bhava I got in the darshan line, and as I knelt before Amma she casually waved her hand before my eyes. The ring sparkled on her middle finger, a symbol for my family, which I felt was resting in her hands, under her protection.

After that I meditated for a long time near Amma. The various stages of my life passed by in my mind, and I could see the garden of my life full of sunflowers and weeds that I personally had planted. A cooling veil of forgiveness and acceptance fell over my joys and sorrows. I realized how little control I had over my own life, which was in reality steered by a mighty timeless power. My thoughts gradually subsided and I sat still, gazing at Amma, who, through her embrace, touched the Love and Light in the hearts of the multitudes who came into her arms.

A month later I went on the Europe Tour with Amma. In those days the halls and our tour groups were small. Usually we were all accommodated along with Amma in private homes. The program near Assisi, in Italy, was held in a large house belonging to a spiritual community, and was the highlight of our trip through seven European countries. The large yet cozy stone house lay in the midst of gentle rolling hills covered with gorse shrubs, and warmly received the flood of happy Amma devotees who entered it day after day. Its rooms hummed with life and activity, like a beehive. People worked in the kitchen, inside the house and in the garden, chanting their mantras. A palpable feeling of peace was in the air. It spread like waves in the ether and helped us open our senses to the beauty of nature. We felt a deep sense of gratitude for this time with Amma.

Darshan took place in a roomy white tent. A large bulldozer had been put to work to create a large, square, flat space to put up the tent. In the daytime, during darshan, the sides of the tent were pulled up and afforded Amma a captivating view of the landscape. A southern wind laden with the perfume of wild flowers blew through the tent, cooling the inside, fanning the devotees sitting on the floor and carrying the melody of the bhajans out over the surrounding countryside.

After four days it was time for Amma to travel to the next program, which would be held in the South of France. People sang, laughed and cried, as Amma's caravan started moving. Amma sat in the lead vehicle and offered her hand for a last touch to those she was leaving behind. I stayed in Assisi to clean up in the kitchen and left the next day by train for Paris, where I was asked to help set up the rooms for Amma and her group in a home in the suburbs. What I did not know was that my ring continued to accompany Amma and would sparkle on her finger yet again during the Devi Bhava I would miss in the South of France.

I was not around when Amma blessed everyone with flower petals during that next Devi Bhava. However, as soon as Amma came to Paris with the group, I was told how, towards the end of Devi Bhava, she had accidently thrown the ring along with the flower petals into the crowd. It had been a little too big for her tiny finger. Now the ring was lost and Amma was concerned.

After the Europe tour some of us were allowed to stay with Amma in a small house in Alsace; this house would later become our first ashram in Europe. As I entered the garden next to the house that evening, to my great surprise I saw Amma sitting all by herself under an apple tree. Stillness and peace emanated from her white form and she looked like the personification of the Earth Mother.

This Earth Mother smiled at me and waved with her hands to come closer. Shyly I sat down in front of her on the grass. After a while a few others joined us and Amma broke the stillness and said she would like to tell us a story.

A swami translated her words as she began: "One of you had given Amma a wonderful ring. This piece of jewelry was not just made of gold and precious stones. It also contained the heart of this person, and along with the ring she also gave Amma her heart. But what did Amma do? She lost it!" Here Amma paused the narration, her face wore a dramatic expression, but she soon smiled and continued: "Amma is very happy because the ring was found amidst the thousands of petals on the floor in the darshan hall, and now that heart is again very close to Amma."

The next day at the airport someone placed the ring in my hands, saying: "Here is your ring." "My ring?" I asked myself. For me the ring had a different meaning, a deeper meaning than just an object of metal and precious stones. Amma had seen my heart in this ring and accepted it. I quietly brought it to Swamini for

sale. What else could I do? How could I possibly give Amma my heart yet a second time?

Six months later I sat in the darshan hall in Amma's ashram in La Reunion, surrounded by dozens of ladies from the island who helped me place *vibhuti*, (sacred ash), in small packets printed with the ashram logo. We worked carefully and joyously, imagining how Amma would soon hold the fruits of our labor in her hand and bless devotees with it. We could experience being close to Amma while we did this seva. In the middle of my work I suddenly had to stop what I was doing. My eyes could not believe what I saw. One of the women in our circle was wearing the ring. It was without a doubt my ring. Astonished and happy, I followed the movements of that dainty hand as it poured the grey vibhuti into the tiny packet with a small spoon. I soaked in the brilliance of the sapphire and diamonds, and without giving away my secret, I turned to my helper and told her: "That is a gorgeous ring you are wearing."

Two happy eyes looked back at me and she replied with a laugh: "Yes, it is really beautiful. Imagine this, my husband told me that Amma has actually worn this ring. It is his gift to me on the birth of our first child!"

I laughed and continued working, amazed at the story of the ring, which I am sure continues even today.

27

AMMA'S CARDS

Call, without expectations
Be the CALL
Then I am here.

Prabha

I was often the official photographer during the marriage ceremonies when Amma would bless the bridal couple with a traditional ritual. It was always a colorful celebration, and in spite of the fixed sequence of events, always new and personal for each wedding. At the beginning of this story, Amma married a couple from Trivandrum, and after some days I took the pictures up to her for approval. She paused while looking at them, picked one out of the bundle and said: "I would like this to be sold in the Ashram store."

She showed me the photo of an introverted Amma, sitting with eyes closed in eternal peace. Her open hands were full of white petals, and a white *mala*, or garland, formed a heart on her bosom. What did Amma see in this picture that I could not? She knew that pictures with the 'direct look,' with Amma looking one

directly in the eyes, sold the most. The bookstall never chose any pictures of her with eyes closed, and in spite of Amma's wish this picture was vehemently rejected.

Nevertheless, I made a copy and placed it in my photo file where it lay for many years. It was never, ever selected for any publication. Almost fifteen years later, when I was selecting pictures for a set of cards I was designing to sell on Amma's foreign tours, I purposely chose that picture because I remembered how precious it had been for Amma.

When I look at this picture today, I am reminded of Amma's prayer for peace and harmony in the world. During the chanting of the Sanskrit words *"Lokah samastah sukhino bhavantu,"* (may all beings in all worlds be happy and at peace), Amma asks us to visualize white flowers of peace falling from the sky down onto the earth. We visualize them falling on mountains, valleys, forests, lakes, on every animal and every human being. Does Amma not look in this picture like the goddess of peace herself, ready to shower the white flowers in her hands over the whole world?

A second picture of personal significance for me also found its way into the set of cards. It was the first of my photos in which I could discover in Amma's gaze the unending reality of the one Truth. I saw these eyes during a lunch break on a North India Tour, when the tour group was resting around Amma in a forest of rubber trees. For me this was the picture of a *mahatma*, absorbed in Brahma Lokah, the realm of the Divine.

In the summer of 2010, my project with the cards was almost finished, and I was able to send the entire package with an acquaintance to America where Amma was on tour. The cards never came back, but Amma's approval for the project reached me. I was happy and inspired to put the finishing touches to my work. In the fall, another copy was ready and accompanied me on the Europe Tour with Amma. There, one day, I showed it to Swamiji for his approval. He took a quick look at my work and asked me if Amma's original sayings were written on the cards, as implied in the index. I replied in the negative, explaining that

I had reread all of Ammas's books, reflected over her teachings, and designed the cards keeping Amma's Western children in mind. At this point he did not believe that Amma had blessed and approved the cards in America. He took the set with him to show to her again.

I do admit with shame that when he doubted whether Amma had approved the cards, I responded with a lot of negative thoughts. To tell you the truth, for some reason I thought he would come back and say 'no'.

The same evening, while I was working on my computer, Swamiji unexpectedly stopped by before Amma came for bhajans and

satsang. He laid the case decorated with lotus blossoms in front of me on the table and said congenially, "Amma wants these cards, and she has a favorite. Open the box. It is the first one on top."

I opened the case slowly, reverentially, and a wave of happiness washed over me. She had really seen them! I knew because her favorite card was the picture that she had liked fifteen years ago, and asked to be sold at the Indian store in the ashram. What Grace! Amma had heard me, had detected my negativity, recognized my doubts and accepted my work in its entirety. Her selection of that picture was like a secret code between the two of us.

"Prabha!" Swamiji's voice took me out of my daydreams, "Amma has a second favorite card. It is under the first one."

When I slowly lifted up the first card my eyes filled with tears. There lay my own favorite card. I was filled with gratitude. Did Amma arrange that entire scenario with Swamiji just to make me more aware of her constant Presence? Did she want to show me again a glimpse of the Truth that my mind will never be able to comprehend in its infinity?

Words of Robert Adams came in my mind:

"You should know that everything that the Master does, he does only for your Self-Realization. It is entirely up to you to know, feel and understand this. Never think that the Master thinks like you or does anything the way you would do it. The wise one only appears to be a normal person like you, but the similarity ends there. Therefore, do not try to understand the wise one and their methods. Just love him/her; that is all you have to do."

28

A PLAY

You see the world according to your perceptions.

Amma

We can learn from even the most insignificant things in life if we view them in the correct perspective. I used to have long, henna red hair when I met Amma for the first time at her program in the mountains of Switzerland. It was my trademark. I was "the tall one with the fiery hair." As a young woman I had modeled for a famous French designer. In those days I could easily slip into any designer outfit, hairdressers to the stars would fix my hair, and I would model these outrageously expensive creations to the interested public.

But then came my draw to Amma's ashram. I was then 47, my daughters almost twenty. I was employed as a teacher at a music school and made all kinds of bamboo flutes. It was obvious to me (although Amma opens her arms without hesitation to all types of people) that I could not show up at Amma's ashram in India with fire-red hair. I wanted to be simple and blend in with the crowd, not stick out like a sore thumb.

It was with this in mind that I made an appointment with a girlfriend for a haircut in her tiny alpine hut high up in the

Before I met Amma, working as a flute maker

mountains near the snow line, where cows grazed on the vast, grassy meadows, and jackdaws circled in the sky. We built a huge fire next to the hut. I wanted to make a ritual offering of my hair in this fire, and along with it everything that would be an obstacle to my spiritual evolution in India. My friend was a chic, self-taught hairdresser, and soon I could feel the cool mountain breezes wafting through my short hair, trying in vain to find long strands they could toss around and play with.

My long locks were being consumed by the fire, and we watched in astonishment at the amount of life force hidden in my hair. The fire crackled and sparked, the flames jumped up high, and soon my hair was reduced to ashes. What a process of transformation, I thought to myself. Soon I was dreaming about my future days in the ashram, where all the burdens I was carrying within me from old habits and impressions would be burnt just as easily in Amma's divine fire. Little did I realize then that this process would not be as painless as cutting off and burning my hair.

It was thus that I arrived in India with short hair dusted with a sprinkling of grey. Despite my careful preparations, I was the pale outsider next to the Indian women with their long black hair worn in a braid or twisted up into a bun. After a few months even my greying hair grew back to its old proud length and I could easily braid it or make a bun. Without a hair dryer or mirror at my disposal I walked around the ashram with my hair sometimes hanging wet, sometimes hastily braided or put up. Needless to say, contrary to my expectations, the length of my hair had nothing to do with my exciting life in the ashram.

After many carefree hair days, I met a woman with a bob cut who moved into the ashram. Her hair was fully grey, cut really short, and I found it wonderful. It reminded me of freedom and being unbound. By then I had reconciled myself to the fact that even with long braided hair there was no way I would ever become fully integrated into the Indian culture, and I begun to again dream of short hair.

The Indian girls assured me, though, that long hair functioned as an antenna for invisible energies and that it would connect me

to highly sensitive powers. Too bad they were unable to convince me, and one day when Amma was in Australia, I made my way to my friend with the bob cut who doubled as my hairdresser this time. I was relieved of my long tresses and just plain relieved that I liked what I saw in the mirror. Unfortunately, only a few of my Western sisters agreed with me.

My Indian sisters were horrified. They were convinced that Amma would dislike my new do. Yes, maybe even take me to task. I knew from experience that Amma does care about our attitude toward our body. She likes us to look after it, keep it healthy through yoga, clothe it simply in clean clothes and do all of this without wasting time. Amma herself is always perfectly dressed, even though the cut, material and white color of her outfit has remained unchanged since the day I met her in 1989. It consists of a simple white dress pleated at the waist, a sleeveless robe worn underneath and a long, gossamer thin piece of white fabric, a half-sari, worn wrapped around the dress.

Before I met Amma, a clairvoyant from England had prophesied that I would marry someone in uniform. I vehemently resisted her suggestion and told that lovely woman that I would most

definitely not be doing anything of the sort. In my mind's eye I could picture a long row of soldiers, policemen, porters, church officials and other uniformed personnel who paraded before me in their official robes, and my level of fascination and enthusiasm remained at zero. Although it turned out that I never did marry anyone from the above list, I did form the first true partnership of my life with a being in 'uniform – Amma. Her flowing robes are a part of her earthly attire and thousands of people have buried themselves in its soft folds for a comforting hug.

When Amma came back home to Amritapuri from Australia I stood with several others near her house. I had found a tiny niche on the small steps of the water tank, and gazed longingly at the corner around which Amma would appear after having walked from the backwater jetty along a path lined by eagerly waiting devotees. Unlike many others who were waiting for Amma to scold me about my haircut, I had completely forgotten the entire matter. My eyes were fixed on the spot where Amma would appear. I had missed her sorely and an expectant joy filled my heart. Then, there she was! She looked straight at me and said loudly in her deep voice: "Prabha, too many photographers in Australia. Click, click, click, No good!" As she walked by I asked, "Were the pictures at least any good?" Amma shrugged her shoulders and grimaced, "I don't know."

Can you imagine what a crazy game of countless projections Amma had set in motion with this little scene that she played with me? Hundreds of women who had been waiting and watching in anticipation of a comment about my hair, saw us exchange words and interpreted both Amma's words and gestures as a rejection of my haircut without understanding a single word of what was said. I was accosted from all sides as soon as Amma went into her room. Everyone projected their own version onto the exchange between Amma and me. I saw on a small scale what the masters mean when they say: "Life is not really as it appears to you. What you see is a projection of your mind."

Amma walking by

My life is also playing out on this stage. It is a movie that flashes on the white screen of pure consciousness, which is my true nature. Amma defines my path of service, love and acceptance in this movie through her pure love and teachings. By seeing my life as a play in the universal consciousness that envelops me, I am able to move forward towards truth and bliss. Amma asks us simply to be. Be as we are, innocent as a child, instead of thinking how we should be. Be, without wanting to understand everything, knowing in our heart that we are a spark of the light of God.

"She was a model in Paris," said Amma one day to those standing around her, "and now she is modeling only for God!"

29

LESSONS IN DETACHMENT

My mind babbles in an endless stream.
Borrowed babbling of humanity. My own words drown.
Thoughts pull me under into the senseless stupor of slumber,
And I am cut asunder from you.

Prabha

When you take a step back, you see things from a different perspective from when they dance right under your nose. In the empty space between you and the situation, your vision is able to expand and grow. Being relaxed and letting go is what Amma calls this way of facing situations. The distance that we are able to create allows us to act, rather than react, in each and every situation. Thus we eventually become observers of everything in our life. It took several lessons from Amma to activate the observer in me – and I am still practicing this art. From childhood, I had been used to reacting with lightning speed to every situation, either to take shelter behind defensive barricades or to launch an attack. In this way, my ego decided my path for me, and I was fully manipulated by it and completely in its hands.

I was living in the ashram when my daughter, Lisa, turned twenty in 1991. To celebrate the occasion, I wanted to create a special card for Amma. I rifled through my collection of pictures to find just the right one. Without a computer or Photoshop, the card had to be done entirely by hand. I was finally satisfied when

I created one that showed Lisa sitting next to Amma on a white lotus blossom and gazing out at me. Now I had only to write down something for Amma in Malayalam. I sought the help of an Indian woman, asking her to write the following words on the back of my card: "Dear Amma, This is my daughter. She turns twenty today. Please bless her."

Amma was already seated on her cot in the darshan hut when I walked in through the back door. An older Indian gentleman was singing poignant bhajans to Lord Krishna, to the accompaniment of the harmonium. His soft yet impressive voice filled the room and touched the hearts of the devotees who were quietly moving forward one after the other into Amma's arms.

Soon I, too, was kneeling in front of her. Holding my card out to her with such fervor that it might have been my twenty-year old daughter herself, I sank into Amma's loving embrace. Feeling completely secure, I imagined how Amma would look at the picture on the card, how she would gaze directly into my little Lisa's heart and make her feel her blessings.

I was suddenly torn out of my daydream when Amma let go of me, waved the picture under my nose and asked me in

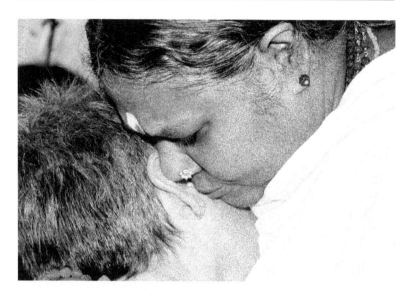

a no-nonsense tone of voice: "Prabha, who is this lady?" I was shocked. I did not understand the world any more. In a fraction of a second Amma had destroyed my entire birthday scenario. Speechless, I sank into a self-destructive abyss. Did she not read the card? Not understand it? Not see it? Oh God, what was wrong? The choice of words? The picture? The entire world? Or Amma? I knelt before her as if rooted to the spot without being able to move or utter a single word. I felt how Amma gently yet firmly pushed me away from her. With shaking steps I walked outside, sat down on the sand, leaned against the wooden walls of the hut and howled with pain. I cried in utter confusion till my inner agony at what had just transpired was transformed into peace.

Stillness spread over my tormented soul, and in this stillness I was able to perceive the transformation that Amma's words had brought to my relationship with Lisa. She had changed my perspective and for the first time I saw my daughter as an independent young woman, embarking upon her journey in life, rather than mainly as my child. Amma had cut the no longer appropriate umbilical cord that still bound me to my daughter by parading my emotional attachment to her before my eyes. This attachment was no longer appropriate for my current situation and aspirations nor for my daughter's. In her unique way she helped me let go, gave me the chance to place my daughter's welfare in her own hands, and in the hands of life itself.

Amma is always working on me, not only when I am in her physical presence. A similar situation played out years later in my family's vacation house by the Italian Riviera. I was spending some days there in the summer with my father, who was at the time 90 years old; Amma was on tour in America. He was taking blood thinners to help with some health issue. All his life, my father had the habit of doing dangerous, adventurous things to attract my attention. I would hover around him with anxiety and beg him to stop. I suppose he felt loved and cared for whenever I did this, because he would often repeat this behavior. This time I discovered him in shorts, standing beside the royal agaves that grew in a corner of the garden. He wanted to cut down one of these large thorny cactus plants with a saw. Anyone acquainted with this huge plant knows how sharp, dangerous and poisonous the large thorns at the end of the fleshy leaves are. My father's bare legs, covered with blue veins were millimeters away from these thorns.

After I saw this, everything played out according to the old pattern. I lost myself in fear for my father. In a millisecond my mind created several scenes of possible accidents, and I cried out, "Please come back right now! Let me take care of that. Get away from that dangerous job." My pulse was racing, but my father only laughed. I fled into the house and buried myself in a large armchair and tried to calm myself. I grabbed an archana book and spoke out loud to Amma: "Amma, for years I have been trying to be composed and detached, but I am failing miserably. I am helpless when my father makes me feel anxious like this. What is the use of all the teachings? How come you are not helping me?"

To calm myself down I began to recite the Sri Lalitha Sahasranama, the thousand names of the Divine Mother, when I heard a loud voice next to me say: "He is Mr. Gerber." These clear words seeped through my disturbed mind where an operation of sorts took place. In a flash, my emotional tie to my father took on a new perspective, and the anxiety-filled bond that had tied me to him since childhood was cut asunder. My father was now Mr. Gerber, a human being among others, a father among other fathers, a life among other lives. Amma gave me the chance to create distance, to trust, to love my father as he was, to let him do his thing in the garden and let me sit in the armchair and recite the archana. A presence bigger than me filled every corner of that house, hung over the rolling hills and the sea, and in the garden near my father. Her Grace had freed us from our old entanglement. I was feeling at peace, freed from the anxious responsibility I had taken on as a child. I was reciting the mantras as my father came into the house looking totally surprised. He expected me to be out in the garden saving him, but here I was inside the house. Along with me, he, too, was transformed. The old pattern was no longer needed because it made no sense.

We often sat together in silence, enjoying each other's nearness, talking about the old days and our dreams. I recognized that my father suffered because he never understood my life with Amma. Even though he had been in Amma's arms several times and received an apple each time he had darshan, he still said, "I am a materialist, and you are a mystic."

My father passed away three years later. A few days before he left his body, he was able to experience why Amma is the most enriching and important thing that has ever happened to me. She appeared to him one night and made him understand that he, too, was bathed in her Love. He felt the lightness of being, his heart opened to the truth that he would always be secure in peace and love. Shortly after that he breathed his last.

30

BACK TO SWITZERLAND

After seventeen years of living in Amritapuri, I awoke to a silent desire in me; it became stronger and began to take concrete form. I wanted to go back to Switzerland and live there, practicing the values that Amma had taught me during my years with her. I also looked forward to playing grandmother to my grandchildren. I was ready for a physical separation from Amma because I could now feel her presence deep within me. This was the foundation upon which I wanted to launch my new life in Switzerland, safe in the knowledge that I was welcome in Amritapuri at any time with open arms. I planned to start a satsang group in my home city, and Amma made me an instructor of her IAM Meditation course.

That was how I came to stay back in the ashram during Amma's North India Tour and make preparations for this transition back to Switzerland. Among other things, I had to put together articles for worship, and instruments for small pujas and the altar at my new home. I wanted to send my books, videos and a few other belongings via air freight to Switzerland, and take my leave of Amma during my stopover in Delhi where she would be giving a program. The main pujari at the ashram helped me choose a brass plate for the arati (the ritual waving of a flame at the end of a puja, with camphor being burned as an offering). He also gave me several articles for the puja that had been used in the Kalari for a long time, and were suffused with the energy of that very special place. A brahmacharini parted with the bell she had used for several months during the daily prayers as the priestess in one of the Brahmasthanam temples consecrated by Amma.

Now what remained was to learn the art of using these items correctly during the arati. I had to practice ringing the bell with the left hand and simultaneously, with my right hand, wave the arati plate with the burning camphor in a clockwise direction around Amma's picture. I practiced this for days in front of the tiny altar in my room next to the Kali shrine, at the same time that the arati was being sung in the temple below.

As planned, I went to meet Amma during my stopover in Delhi. A huge mass of humanity overflowed from the ashram located in the suburbs of Delhi.

A Brahmasthanam Temple designed by Amma, where the deity was consecrated and installed by her, was the center of this holy place. Several pujas are conducted daily at the ashram, and many of Amma's charitable projects have also been initiated there. As it got dark, I sat quietly by myself on the flat roof of the ashram building, thinking about my departure and new beginning. I could hear the noise of the city nearby: car horns, the roar of motors, and from a distance, the howling of a pack of stray dogs.

Saturn Puja

And here I was sitting in heavenly peace right in the middle of the nocturnal noise of the big city!

The evening was cool. Below me on the ashram grounds glowed countless flickering oil lamps amidst a sea of colorful saris. Hundreds of people sitting close to one another concentrated on conducting a soul-stirring ritual lead by Amma. They were forgetting themselves in the moment, and their very presence seemed to be a prayer. An indescribable beauty, simplicity and light spread over the oil lamps and the crowd. Then, her voice pierced the night and the foggy curtain of pollution that hid the

stars. Amma sang: "Bhakti do Jagadambe, Prem do Jagadambe." Her words meant, "Grant me devotion, divine Mother, grant me Love." A growing energy field spread outward from Amma. It offered healing and receptivity so that love and compassion could awaken in human hearts.

After waiting in line for a long time, I finally stood before Amma to receive my darshan before leaving for Switzerland. She was happy to see me and grabbed the small bell that I held out to her, kissed it and began ringing it. Just as I had, she waved the make-believe arati tray with her right hand, doing the arati in front of me just as I had practiced for many evenings in front of my altar in the ashram.

I was moved, witnessing this, and following an impulse I gently removed the bell from Amma's hand. It was now my turn to do arati. I rang the bell steadily with my left hand and my right hand mimed the movement of the arati tray with the imaginary flame, as it circled higher and higher around Amma and above her head.

In that moment I could feel that Amma was the divine energy that suffused everything on this earth, filled the entire universe, and that had neither beginning nor end. "Ho, ho, ho," said Amma, bringing me back down to earth, and I slowly returned the bell and tray to her lap. This was my farewell to Amma.

After this amazing blessing I flew back to Switzerland to begin the next stage of my life. The arati flame accompanied me to my new beginnings. I felt myself carried in the arms of Love, which had built a precious space in me, a kind of a treasure trove containing a priceless diamond that gave my life direction and purpose. I knew, then, that the real darshan has always to take place inside of me.

True freedom lies
BEHIND the stories
Written by life.

Prabha

31

THE STATUE

The ego is a veil that covers the inner teacher.
However, when you discover this teacher in you,
you will encounter him everywhere in creation.
He will show you that you are part of the whole.
Every grain of sand, every thorn,
every wave in the river will serve
to make you aware of this.

Amma

The scriptures say that a real seeker sees the entire world as the Master's body and is always ready to serve one and all. What does Amma see when she serves us the whole day, when she looks at our bodies? Amma sees everything that we see, but simultaneously she also sees *through* everything. What Amma sees is not comprehensible to our rational mind. Amma's seeing arises directly from stillness.

In a message she gave us from this exalted perspective, Amma said:

"Everything in the world exists to teach you. Life is like a grindstone against which your ego is rubbed down so that the wonderful diamond inside us may shine forth. This diamond is your true nature, is divine Consciousness. Therefore, live each day with renewed effort to seek the silence and stillness behind the chattering mind. Amma gives you many tests so that you may shine more from your inner self. Unfortunately, you fail in almost all these

tests, because Amma's tests are not merely written down on paper like at the university. These tests are created by life itself. Think that it could be a test from Amma when anger arises in you or you lose your patience."

Not long ago, after my return to life in Switzerland, Amma sent me just such a test in the form of a large wire statue that showed up one day on my neighbor's balcony.

"Oh, no!" was my first thought when I saw this lady made of metal wires one morning as I sat for meditation. "This monstrous thing is ruining my view, covering a large piece of the beautiful sky, and it is so out of place amidst the natural beauty surrounding me. How sad and how stupid!"

My meditations during the next few days were devoted to this unwanted guest on my neighbor's balcony rather than to discovering my true essence. My thoughts were rebellious and persisted on flying to the neighbor's balcony. My mind was so out of control that I could not help being aware of its turbulence.

Both astonished and ashamed, I admitted to myself that a few pieces of metal wire put together could fully ruin my concentration.

"Novice," I said to myself, part jokingly and part in earnest, "you fell into the trap, and your ego celebrates!" I imagined how Amma would laugh about me, but still love me. Suddenly I had an idea. Why not turn the tall, lonely lady on my neighbor's balcony into Amma? Amma, who is looking into my apartment and the river that flows below, Amma, who has moved in under Bern's grey winter sky.

As soon as I christened my new neighbor as Amma my entire morning ritual changed. Amma was near me, she was watching me through the window and sending her smile into my room. I began to integrate the statue standing in the cold winter air into my life, began to love her and use her as support for concentration during my meditation.

One day, when I woke up early as usual, I perceived an unusual light in the semi-darkness of dawn. As it became brighter with daybreak, I could see roofs covered in snow and the branches of the trees in the garden decked out in white. My joy had no bounds as I gazed upon 'Amma' later from my seat on the meditation cushion. Winter had placed a white snow-scarf around her shoulders and a cute hat on her head. Our time together was such a blessing during the next few days! The wire statue that had caused so much disturbance in my mind was now my quiet companion, a transformation brought about just by my shifting my perspective. Soon, in February, I parted from this companion to travel to Amma's ashram in India.

I returned from India one night that same spring, and looked forward to seeing Amma waiting on the balcony when I sat down for meditation the next morning. What a shock I got. She had disappeared. Her absence felt like a sharp pain. I felt disappointed and let down because she left behind a big gap in my daily schedule. And what did my steady companion, my mind, do then? It bitterly bemoaned the loss of this piece of art, just as it had hated its presence when the statue first appeared. Was I totally crazy? I could hear Amma laughing heartily at my foolishness. I agreed with her and began also to laugh at the great joker in my head – my mind.

Because of this mind, Amma has presented me with countless tests. Every test helps me convert the backpack of my ego into a float to help me swim. This float carries me through the ocean of life, and I am learning like a good swimmer to play with the waves and enjoy myself as I am carried along by it. I am learning to be a swimmer who loves the ocean and waves, can withstand a storm, and continues to hope that the trickster mind will finally become a willing servant. This servant will one day learn to wait outside when the stillness in me opens up. This story shows that every experience can enrich us when viewed through the right lens. One thing is sure: my treasure hides behind the façade of the ego. To discover it I need Amma, who will help me choose the correct pair of glasses and teach me how to have a clear vision of this world

32

GOLD NUGGETS

Come my Amma of deepest dark hue,
Come my Amma of love-longing still new,
Laugh with me, weep with me,
Give me your hand.
In the lap of your Being
I am transformed beyond me,
In the boundlessness of your Self
I am blessed to eternity.

Prabha

Why do thousands of people all over the world try to integrate Amma's words and her spiritual teachings into their lives? How come we feel attracted to her like iron filings to a magnet? I don't want to bore you with any kind of clichéd answer to this question. How can anyone understand the mystery that is Amma without becoming it themselves? However, I remember Amma often saying that life is a play. I love games, especially mysterious ones. This reminds me of a story.

I am looking on as my grandchild plays with a toy. It consists of tiny multicolored buttons. She has discovered that they are attached to magnets that can either attract or repel each other. Deeply engrossed in her discovery, I hear her say, "This here is a north pole; this is a south pole." I watch with fascination as she finds out that like poles repel and opposite poles attract. In my mind's eye, I picture a glowing pole that has both opposites of north and south integrated in it. It continuously sends out waves of love, peace and compassion for all human beings.

This pole is Amma, and I see a small spark of her in each person. No wonder that we are all so attracted to her. She brings out the best in us when she says:

> *"The most important goal of your life is to find the treasure of eternal truth and permanent peace in your heart. If you look for this treasure on the outside, it will be like emptying the ocean to catch a fish. The treasure of lasting peace can only be found on the inside."*

This is why we are all treasure seekers, gold diggers in our inner selves. We dust off old cobwebs which really don't belong to us, get rid of habits and conditionings, dig and search with great concentration, and focus like the gold diggers in old American movies. If we keep at it, occasionally we can find tiny nuggets of gold that give us the hope and inspiration to continue digging, to continue believing in the gold mine.

Amma is a master at distributing this golden treasure. Every now and then she gives us a glimpse of this priceless metal so that we may keep walking towards the treasure trove within. She is most happy when we are able to integrate what we find into our lives and let it shine there.

One of my gold-nugget stories began when Amma started scolding me one Devi Bhava night during the Europe Tour. I stood beside her chair to seat the people next to her, where they would receive a mantra from Amma. As soon as Amma was ready to give the mantra, I would whisper the devotee's preferred form of God in her ear. I had been doing this seva about half an hour and I had been really messing it up. Amma began to scold me and said something to Geeta, her helper. I could see my downfall coming when Geeta turned to me and said, "Amma says you love it when she scolds you." Amma looked at me questioningly as she held a woman in her arms, and I had a flashback of the hundreds of situations when Amma had scolded me. Yes, actually I had started my career as a photographer with Amma saying to me, "You can be my photographer and you must continue your work even if I scold you." So I had indeed been forewarned, and a scolding from Amma had come to be a kind of intimate contact between us. I replied to Geeta, "I like Amma's scolding because at least this way she speaks to me directly and personally."

Geeta translated and Amma smiled, saying, "Prabha spring loose!" which more or less meant that I was a little crazy. Encouraged, I replied, "Amma, in my next life I want to speak the same language as you."

The translations went on back and forth, and as Amma looked at me with eyes full of love, Geeta said, "Amma says her language is the language of the heart. Once you learn to speak this language, every other language will lose its importance for you." Amma made me very happy with this exchange. She had just thrown a gold nugget on my path. I had suffered because of the language barrier and my inability to learn Amma's native language, Malayalam. All that pain dissolved in the language of the heart that does not consist of words.

Yet another 'gold nugget' story happened not too long after this one, during one of my stays in India. I hoped to spend some quiet time in the ashram. There were no inner conflicts, no jealousies or moments of feeling inferior that crept up insidiously to ruin my peace. Even then, after four weeks of darshan abstinence, I began to sing the same old song of jealousy towards all these Indians who were able to talk and laugh so easily with Amma.

I decided to go for darshan. After receiving my token, I sat in the darshan line, which took its own sweet time to move towards Amma. Instead of letting myself be distracted by the various tests that only someone waiting in line for darshan knows about, I thought about the wonderful experience with Amma waiting for me at the other end of the line.

Closing my eyes, I whispered to myself, "Only Amma and I, only Amma and I." In this way I crossed all the hurdles without any distracting thoughts – even the hurdle where I had to wipe

Darshan

my face with half a tissue! At last I made it quite close to Amma. But then I was suddenly asked, "Prabha, which language do you speak?" I answered quite spontaneously without looking up or thinking, "Everything except German."

A second later I disappeared into Amma's arms and heard her whisper: "Ma, ma, maaa, mole, mole, mole, my daughter, my daughter, my daughter, darling, darling, darling." By the time Amma reached "ma chérie, ma chérie," I had dissolved in laughter.

She released me from her embrace and her eyes, too, were laughing as she asked me something. After my answer, Amma again pulled me to her and whispered some more questions in my ear. I answered in her ear, then asked her a question. Amma whispered in my other ear and this went on back and forth just as I had seen her do with Indians speaking Malayalam. Only, do not ask me in what language we spoke. It must have definitely been the language of the heart because I experienced neither shyness nor hesitation. I was simply surrendered to this wonderful sense of intimacy.

My feet barely touched the earth as I left, with holy ash, candy and a banana in my hand. As I shakily made my way to sit on a stool, those sitting around Amma asked me, "In which language did you speak to Amma? I, too, have longed to talk to her like that." I sat down in the back of the stage, closed my eyes and repeated: "Only Amma and I" in order to ground myself. Eating the prasad candy did not help much. Only after I ate the banana was I able to finally open my eyes and walk off the stage into the hall.

I had not expected that so many people who had watched my darshan would stop me and ask for the details. Thanks to all the large screen televisions, everyone sitting in the hall who had been completely focused on Amma had seen everything. To escape all the questions, I decided to take my banana peel, which had passed through Amma's sacred hands, to one of the ashram cows. I just could not bring myself to throw the peel into the designated container marked for food waste. Incredibly, someone who walked with the help of a cane followed me all the way to the cowshed to quiz me about my darshan. I told her, just as I had told the others, that the conversation was private, which was why Amma had whispered in my ears.

The Western cowherd, who was working by the feeding trough, could hardly believe his eyes when he saw me show up with the tiny banana peel. He directed me to the biggest cow. Still under the influence of Amma's 'golden nugget,' I approached the cow without fear and she took the yellow peel from my hands. Then I hid myself on the roof of the temple to be alone with my joy.

As time passed I could see how Amma had adroitly used our 'conversation' not only to work on me, but also on hundreds of others who were watching. She had skillfully built up the 'whispering in the ear' scenario so that she could touch as many people in as many inner situations as possible. This way she reached into their souls and opened their eyes to the personal obstacles that lay on their path to the golden treasure. When Amma works with us as we walk the path, I don't think that she simply wipes away one or several problems for each of us individuals. Rather, through her presence and her actions, she initiates the process of becoming aware of these obstacles. She picks up these problems and places them beside us so that we are no longer trapped inside of them but have the breathing space to turn and observe them. In this way our obstacles and shortcomings become a rich field for practicing spiritual teachings, where we can work on them, try different solutions, and grow.

Amma says:

"Only a person who is open for the Truth of the Self can be truly happy. Whoever can be one with whatever life brings, towards that person come God's grace and teachings in a flowing dance."

And believe me, such a person will now and again find golden nuggets strewn on his or her path. Such nuggets can be found everywhere, not only near Amma's physical form. They may surprise us during a walk in the city, in the streetcar, at work, while hiking up a steep hill or gazing at the star-studded skies. They are always there in every corner of the world. You can find them wherever you are completely present: in the fields, the woods, mountains and valleys, in oases and in the desert. This is because Amma's gold is everywhere, strewn over the entire universe.

Amma and I took this picture together

Amma called me to where she was standing on the steps leading to her room. Then she pointed to the sea of laughing faces at the bottom of the stairs, took my camera and held it in front of my eyes. I had to focus and click and this is the result!

33

EPILOGUE

Dear Readers,

I have shared parts of my life and many of my very personal experiences with Amma in the pages of this book. My goal was to give you glimpses of my early years spent in the Ashram with Amma through pictures and stories, and to share how Amma worked with me and continues to work with me on my path to the freedom of the Self.

I would like to reiterate that my words do not in any way try to define what Amma is. Amma herself has said: "If you would like to know me, then you must become me."

I think that each person sees Amma through his or her own personal vision and perspective. All people have their very own pictures of Amma, their very own way of relating to her. Deep in our hearts, though, for all of us, she is the very same essence. She is the divine Consciousness that lives in us, waiting to shine forth.

The Master is like a river. Once you jump into this river, the current will inexorably take you to the sea. It takes courage to jump into a flowing river and the river will not force you to do so. It is simply there, flowing and accepting.

Amma

May we all flow towards the light of Truth that shines in our hearts. May divine Grace and Amma's Love always be with us on our journey.

Om Amriteshwaryai Namah

GLOSSARY

ACCHAMMA – grandmother, mother of the father

ACCHAN – father in Malayalam, the language of Kerala

AMRITAPURI – Amma's main ashram headquarters located at Amma's birthplace in Kerala, India

ARATI – Traditionally performed near the end of a ritual worship. Consists of waving burning camphor before the object of worship. Arati symbolizes surrender. Just as the camphor burns away without a trace, so does the ego dissolve in the process of surrendering to the guru or to God.

ARCHANA – 'Offering for worship;' a form of worship in which the names of a deity are chanted, usually 108, 300 or 1,000 names in one sitting.

ASHRAM – 'Place of striving;' a place where spiritual aspirants live or visit in order to lead a spiritual life and engage in spiritual practice. It is usually the home of a spiritual master, saint or ascetic, who guides the aspirants.

AUM (also OM) – According to the Vedic scriptures, this is the primordial sound in the universe and the seed of creation. All other sounds arise out of AUM and resolve back into AUM.

BHAJAN – Devotional song; devotional singing

BHAVA – Divine mood, attitude or state

BRAHMACHARI (masc.)/ BRAHMACHARINI (fem.) – A celibate disciple who practices spiritual disciplines under a master.

DARSHAN – An audience with or a vision of the Divine or a holy person

DEVI BHAVA – Divine mood, the state in which Amma reveals her oneness with the Divine Mother

DHOTI – Piece of cloth wrapped around the waist, worn by men

HOMA – Sacred fire ritual

KALARI – The small temple where Amma used to hold Krishna and Devi Bhava darshans in the early days of the ashram and where daily pujas are still conducted.

KALI – 'The Dark One,' a form of the Divine Mother. She may seem frightening because she destroys the ego.

KARTHIKA – Amma's birth star

KRISHNA BHAVA – the state in which Amma revealed her oneness with Krishna.

LEELA – divine play

MAHATMA – Great soul. When Amma uses the word '*mahatma*,' she is referring to a Self-realized soul.

MANTRA – Sacred formula or prayer, which is repeated as often as possible. A tool to awaken one's concentration and dormant spiritual power.

MURTI – devotional statue for worship

NAMAHA – Sanskrit, 'I bow down'

Peetham – Seat

PRASAD – Blessed offering or a gift from the hand of a master.

PUJA – Ritual

PUJARI – Person who performs a ritual.

SAMADHI – Oneness with God. A transcendental state in which one loses all sense of individual identity.

SANKALPA – divine resolve

SATSANG – Being in the company of a mahatma or listening to a spiritual talk or discussion.

SEVA – selfless service

SRI LALITHA SAHASRANAMA – the 1000 names of Devi, the Divine Mother

VASANA – latent tendencies or subtle desires within the mind which manifest as action and habits.

VIBHUTI – sacred ash

CPSIA information can be obtained
at www.ICGtesting.com
Printed in the USA
BVHW08s1956280618
520364BV00009B/107/P

9 781680 377453